TWAYNE'S WORLD AUTHORS SERIES

A Survey of the World's Literature

Sylvia E. Bowman, Indiana University

GENERAL EDITOR

FRANCE

Maxwell A. Smith, Guerry Professor of French, Emeritus
The University of Chattanooga
Visiting Professor in Modern Languages
The Florida State University

EDITOR

Jean Giono

(*TWAS 7*)

TWAYNE'S WORLD AUTHORS SERIES (TWAS)

The purpose of TWAS is to survey the major writers —novelists, dramatists, historians, poets, philosophers, and critics—of the nations of the world. Among the national literatures covered are those of Australia, Canada, China, Eastern Europe, France, Germany, Greece, India, Italy, Japan, Latin America, New Zealand, Poland, Russia, Scandinavia, Spain, and the African nations, as well as Hebrew, Yiddish, and Latin Classical literatures. This survey is complemented by Twayne's United States Authors Series and English Authors Series.

The intent of each volume in these series is to present a critical-analytical study of the works of the writer; to include biographical and historical material that may be necessary for understanding, appreciation, and critical appraisal of the writer; and to present all material in clear, concise English—but not to vitiate the scholarly content of the work by doing so.

Jean Giono

By MAXWELL A. SMITH

Guerry Professor of French, Emeritus
The University of Chattanooga
Visiting Professor in Modern Languages
The Florida State University

Twayne Publishers, Inc.   ::   New York

To M. C.

Preface

THE NOVELS of Jean Giono have achieved in many foreign countries an acclaim equal to their enthusiastic reception in France. At least nine of his books have been translated into English and published in Great Britain, the United States, or both. Nevertheless, although seven books have been published about him in French and more are in preparation, nothing longer than an essay has so far appeared about this novelist in English. Professor Henri Peyre has called Giono probably the most original of French writers between the two wars, a great artist "whose appeal is to all modern man, as is Thomas Hardy's or William Faulkner's, even though the setting and the characters of their books are narrowly localized." A recent essay by the distinguished French critic, Robert Kanters, in *Le Figaro Littéraire* confirms Giono's high rank in French literature: "No one contests that he is among the number of our greatest writers, when one counts them, let us say, on the fingers of two hands." And finally that authoritative organ of British literary criticism, the *London Times Literary Supplement*, terms Giono "one of the most prolific and vigorous of contemporary novelists . . . a novelist of the greatest power and invention . . . one of the most important novelists in Europe today." Because of these assessments, a comprehensive introduction in English to Giono's work is well overdue.

The major portion of the material for this book was obtained during the summers of 1957 and 1960 in the Bibliothèque Nationale in Paris and while in residence at Giono's home town of Manosque where frequent consultations with the author and visits to the scenes of his novels were possible. In consulting the multitude of newspapers and magazine articles about Giono in the Bibliothèque Nationale, I received from the former Nazi Occupation authorities the same involuntary cooperation that I had experienced with my earlier study of Saint-Exupéry. To keep as many able-bodied French youths as possible from deportation as workers to Germany, every effort was made by French authorities during the Occupation to find work which would appear to the Nazis as indispensable. Accordingly a number of young men were employed by the National Library to make dossiers of all the articles published on outstanding French authors. As a result I found a fat packet containing every French article which had appeared about Giono from 1929 to 1944.

There remain a few words to say concerning the procedure followed in this study. Several of the excellent French treatises on Giono have chosen to give a brief résumé of his life and then to discuss his work *en bloc*. Since, however, Giono has undergone a series of transformations with significant changes of style and outlook, it has seemed best to follow his development as far as possible in chronological order, with alternating biographical chapters which help to explain these modifications.

No apology is made for the obvious fact that the subject of this study has impressed his biographer as a warmly attractive individual. On the other hand this book is in no wise a panegyric or uncritical eulogy, for I have endeavored to point out the various foibles and weaknesses in the man and in his work which make him a thoroughly human and far from infallible personality. To avoid possible personal bias, I have not hesitated to quote liberally from his critics, both favorable and unfavorable, particularly in regard to his most controversial works.

After some hesitation I felt it best to translate into English the comments of French and Italian critics as well as the quotations from Giono himself. Since the greater part of Giono's masterpieces are available in English, I hope that this introduction to his works will be of value not only to scholars but also to a broader public who may not easily read French and Italian. The quotations from Giono's works are my own translations except in the case of those from *Blue Boy, The Song of the World, The Horseman on the Roof, The Malediction,* and *The Straw Man,* for which the admirable translations of Miss Katherine Clarke, Messrs Fluchère and Myers, Mr. Jonathan Griffin, Mr. Peter de Mendelssohn, and Miss Phillis Johnson, respectively, have been utilized. Several of the chapters in this study have appeared in somewhat different

Preface

form in *Books Abroad, Romance Notes, The French Review,* and
the *Kentucky Foreign Language Quarterly.*

I wish to express a special debt and gratitude to Giono's friend,
the late Lucien Jacques, for his personal reminiscences; to the late
Katherine Clarke, Professor of French at the University of Massa-
chusetts, for her helpful information and encouragement; to
M. and Mme Roger Lévy and M. Bertrand Lévy for their sympathetic interest and for calling my attention to several current
articles of importance; to Dr. Robert Lester and the Southern
Fellowship Fund and to the University of Chattanooga for grants-
in-aid which made this research possible; and, not least, to my
wife, Mary Clyde Smith, for her patience in typing the manuscript
and for her many valuable comments and suggestions about the
text.

MAXWELL A. SMITH

Lookout Mountain, Tennessee

Acknowledgments

I am grateful to the following French and American publishers for their kind permission to quote from books by and about Giono.

From Giono's works: to Éditions Bernard Gresset (Paris) for *Colline, Un de Baumugnes, Regain, Naissance de l'Odyssée, Que ma joie demeure,* and *Mort d'un personnage;* to Editions Gallimard (Paris) for *Le Grand Troupeau, Batailles dans la montagne, Pour Saluer Melville, Un Roi sans divertissement, Noé, Le Bout de la route, Domitien* and *Voyage en Italie;* to Editions du Rocher (Monaco) for *Le Voyage en calèche;* to the Viking Press (New York) for *Blue Boy* and *The Song of the World;* and to Alfred A. Knopf (New York) for *The Horseman on the Roof.*

From works about Giono: to Oxford University Press (New York) for the *Contemporary French Novel* by Henri Peyre; to New Directions (New York) for *The Books in My Life* by Henry Miller; to the University of California Press (Berkeley and Los Angeles) for *Jean Giono et les techniques du roman* by Pierre Robert; to Romée de Villeneuve and Les Presses Universelles (Avignon) for *Jean Giono, ce solitaire* by Romée de Villeneuve; to Les Editions Universitaires (Paris-Bruxelles) for *Jean Giono* by Jacques Pugnet; to Editions du Seuil (Paris) and Georges Borchardt for *Giono peint par lui-même* by Claudine Chonez; and to Editions Gallimard for *Jean Giono et les religions de la terre* by Christian Michelfelder.

Contents

Contents

Chronology

1895   Jean Giono born in Manosque, March 30.

1902–   Schooling in Collège de Manosque.
1911

1906   Summer in Corbières; introduction to nature and to the Classics.

1911   Leaves school to work in the bank, October 28.

1914–   Service as infantry private in World War I. Demobilized
1919   in October, 1919.

1920   Returns from bank in Marseilles to one in Manosque. Death of his father, April 25. Marriage to Elise Maurin, June 22.

1922   Beginning of life-long friendship with Lucien Jacques.

1924   Publication of first "poèmes en prose" as *Accompagnés de la flûte*.

1926   Birth of daughter Aline, October 25.

1928   Grasset rejects manuscript of *Naissance de l'Odyssée* which he is glad to publish in 1930 after Giono became famous.

1929   Publication of *Colline* (first volume of the *Trilogy of Pan*) already made famous the preceding year by Gide's praise when it appeared in the obscure Paris magazine *Commerce*.

1930   Giono resigns from the bank and purchases the home Le Paraïs on the Mont d'Or where he lives today. Receives thousand dollar Prix Brentano for *Colline*. Publication of *Regain*.

1931   Receives Northcliff Prize for *Regain*. Publication of *Le Grand Troupeau*.

1933   Publication of *Jean le bleu* (Blue Boy) and of *Le Serpent d'étoiles*.

Chronology

CHAPTER 1

Manosque, the Man and Family Background

I *His Town*

TO approach Manosque from the north, we can take in Grenoble a little train which huffs and puffs its way in serpentine curves high up through the Alps before it begins to descend into the sun-baked valleys of Provence and along the rushing Durance which has figured in so many of Jean Giono's stories. To the right, extending for many miles, is the somber, forbidding mass of Lure Mountain, the scene of *Colline* and of many other novels of Giono.

According to the Michelin guide, Manosque, a little town of some seven thousand five hundred souls, acquired its surname "la Pudique" (the modest one) from an event connected with the passage of Francis the First through the city in 1516. When the consul's daughter, charged with presenting the keys of the city to the sovereign, made him a complimentary speech, the admiring glances which this gallant king cast at the young lady seem to have alarmed her modesty. To hide the freshness of her complexion and the charms which nature had lavished on her, she exposed her face to sulphurous vapors. Francis, moved by such excessive modesty, then overwhelmed the young lady and her family with his royal favor and generosity. Manosque was also known at one time as "la ville des hirondelles," as we learn in one of the stories in *L'Eau vive* of Giono, because of the presence of swallows in tremendous numbers.

Through a window in the Hotel du Terreau, we view in the distance the soft, swelling slope of the little mountain Toutes Aures (Provençal for "all the winds") and, in the foreground, the terrace of a tiny garden filled with cypresses and miniature palm trees. If we were in the garden we could hear the gentle splash of a fountain. Above the garden is a large public square framed with plane trees where men and boys roll balls in the typical Southern game of *boules*.

The narrow streets of Manosque have changed but little since the Middle Ages. Some evidently were renamed in the eighteenth century for they bear such names as Rue Danton, Rue Voltaire, and Rue J. J. Rousseau. Others apparently take their name from some ancient landmark which has now disappeared, such as the Rue du Moulin (where once stood a mill for pressing olives), Rue du Four-Neuf ("new bake oven"), and the Rue des Carmes (the one-time abode of Carmelite monks). Some street names are highly poetic, such as the Rue du Bon Repos, the Rue d'Aubette (from *aube* meaning "dawn"), and the Rue du Mont d'Or. The Rue Torte (twisted) does not belie its name, and the Rue du Poète actually harbored a Provençal poet. Dating back without doubt to the Middle Ages are the Rue du Palais (a feudal castle once stood near the Hotel du Terreau); the Ruelle des Lices, which evidently led to the site of former tournaments; and the Rue du Jeu de Paume, predecessor of our modern tennis courts. Cool because the sun never penetrates their chasm-like recesses, these streets are so narrow that one must press himself against the wall to allow a motorcycle to pass. Only the boulevards which surround the town in place of the former walls are wide enough for motor traffic.

At the opposite ends of the town are two gate towers that were built in the fourteenth century: the Porte Soubeyran, decorated with stone balustrade and campanile, and the Porte Saunerie, with its two lateral turrets crowned with crenelated battlements. The latter name originated perhaps from the presence of salt dealers in the neighborhood, though Giono has also suggested a slaughter house, since *sauner* in popular language means "to bleed." A tiny square between the Hotel de Ville and the old church of Notre Dame forms the only patch of vacant land in the midst of this tightly built and compressed town, and it is easy to see how Giono's Hussard could have wandered for several days over the rooftops while escaping his pursuers below.

Through the center of the town, from one gate tower to the other, runs the picturesque Grand' Rue, so called because it is exactly nine feet wide while all other streets are only six. It was here that Giono spent his childhood in the vast, dilapidated mansion which housed his mother's laundry on the ground floor and his father's shoe shop on the third. In this street one is at once conscious of being in the South, for the doors of all the shops consist of swishing bead chains for circulation of the air. Outside the city proper lies a tiny *Jardin Public* where in the shade of cypress and palm trees one catches a glimpse of the red-tiled roof of Giono's home nestling on the green slopes of his Mountain of Gold.

II   *First Impressions*

Leaving the town to walk to Giono's house, we found an old, bent peasant splitting faggots whom we asked for directions. His face lighted up with a smile as he said with alacrity: "Oui, je connais ça, c'est mon ami." I suspect we would have had the same answer from any other inhabitant, for every one seemed to know Giono personally and to have read his books, including the proprietor of our hotel. As we climbed the dusty road up the Mont d'Or, framed by high walls shaded by dark green cypress and scrub oak trees, I thought of an amusing article by Marcel Arland in the September, 1953 issue of *Le Figaro Littéraire,* describing his pilgrimage to the house of the novelist:

I asked for directions to his house. "It's up there," they said, "on the mountain." An hour later after many detours, I found myself some ten kilometers distant from the town, still looking for the mountain. A workman stretched out in the shade of a bush explained to me that I had already passed the mountain, that it was behind me (I perceived a swelling of terrain, let's say a hill or a hillock) and that it was easy to find M. Giono's house because it was the last one on the edge of the canal. I came back, left my car, looked for the canal; I looked for a long time, and again I asked for directions. "But there it is, the canal." "Where then?" "Here in front of you at your feet." Indeed, leaning down, I discovered between some high grass and briers a narrow ditch, which moreover was dry. And the next hour, when I had found Giono and told him of my adventures: "Oh," he said with a friendly smile, "people are like that in this country."

When a visitor rings the bell, he is ushered to the third floor to what Giono calls his *phare* or light house, consisting of a low study and library with walls entirely covered by books except for a portrait of Giono's mother. On one table lies an incredible number of pipes and quill pens. Through a dormer window the visitor sees the red-tiled roofs and iron campanile of Manosque, the city which Giono has compared to "a loaf of bread, baked too long

. . . lying on the slope of the hills, at the back of a gulf in the plain." From the other window he sees the Durance River, "like a branch of a fig tree in the plain," and beyond it the plateau of Valensole, "which closes the plain like a bar of old bronze."

Giono, with round face of healthy ruddiness and with the dreamy eyes of a mountaineer, "looking more like a Homeric bard or a biblical prophet than a Parisian man of letters," as a French journalist recently described him, is now well past seventy; but, with a robustness and vivacity which belie his years, he rises from his writing table to greet his guest with a friendly hand-shake. Puffing contentedly on his pipe and speaking in a voice delightfully tinged with Provençal accent, Giono answers with animation and disarming frankness even the most personal and indiscreet questions of his interviewer concerning his background, his family, and his literary plans for the future.

Though Giono seems to feel a nostalgic predilection for his early *Colline,* he prefers his present style which subordinates lyric description of nature to psychological analysis because it forces him to discipline his natural tendency to prolixity. Denying vehemently that he has lost his early optimism and now has a more sober and pessimistic outlook on life, Giono qualified his denial with the admission that he has come to realize he can make only individuals happy—not nations or even large groups.

Few writers today give such an impression of joyful absorption in the writer's craft, or of absolute happiness and contentment in the rustic surroundings of his rose bushes and garden. Impressed with such serenity and confidence in the future—for Giono talks of his plans when, at seventy-five, he hopes to have gained satisfactory mastery of his style—the visitor takes his leave, convinced that Giono's warm human touch and zest for living must make him a fascinating comrade and friend.

III *The Maternal Side*

No writer perhaps has ever been more firmly attached to his ancestors through every fiber of his being than Giono. Three of them—his paternal grandfather, his father, and his mother—appear frequently in his books, sometimes as models for the principal protagonists. Some of the complexities and apparent paradoxes which we shall observe in Giono's personality may be

explained by the mixture of races and cultures found in his for-
bears.

If on his mother's side Giono is of French descent, even here we
see a blend of northern and southern strains. From his maternal
grandmother of solid Picard stock, Giono may well have inherited
his sense of the picturesque and his humor. His maternal grandfather was a Pourcin from Provence, who had worn the red panta-
loons of a Zouave at the battle of Magenta before becoming first
trombone player in the Imperial Band of Napoleon III.

In 1892 their daughter Pauline Pourcin married the elderly Jean-
Antoine Giono, and their only child was Jean Giono, born on
March 30, 1895. Though his mother seems to have had far less
influence than his father on Jean's education and intellectual development, he owes to her nonetheless his extreme sensitivity to
the suffering of others, his early shyness and timidity, his need for
giving and receiving affection. In the recital of his homecoming
from the war in the volume *L'Eau vive* (*Son Dernier Visage*), we
find this debt movingly expressed: "I have inherited from my
mother her blue eyes, her almost blond hair which comes with her
from Picardy, and that distressed sensibility, with a measure of
weakness and lamentation, that skin so lightly pressed on the
heart, the lungs and the liver, that skin so thin that it is no longer
a protection, but only a coating of glue as it were to hold together
my vital organs against the pressure of the world."

But Pauline seems to have been the more practical member of
the family since she managed a laundry with three assistants and
two apprentices; she was always a little reproachful to her husband for his reckless generosity towards waifs and vagabonds. At
the same time, however, she possessed a strain of mystic devout-
ness. She countered her husband's agnosticism with a lifelong ad-
herence to the Catholic faith, as we see for example in the picture
which Giono gives us of her in his story *"Le Poète de la Famille"*
in *L'Eau vive:* "Every Sunday at five minutes to three in the afternoon, just at the moment of leaving for Vespers, a dazzling ver-
tigo passed through the blue eyes of my mother. Immediately she
would put both hands to her temples, arranging the imperturba-
ble equilibrium of her little black hat on her beautiful blond hair,
and she would set forth straightway towards God, her feet placed
on an arrow." Giono was twelve years old at this time.

Perhaps it was the toll of poverty and hard work which wore down her vitality in the end; perhaps it was the strain of living with a husband much older than she, who was as impractical and selfless as a Saint Francis of Assisi but enfeebled and embittered by old age. At any rate, in the story *"Son Dernier Visage"* already referred to, we observe with compassion the change which has occurred in her during Jean's absence at the front: "I could see her well. For the first time I understood her face. . . . Her happiness was over. Ashen hair, a gray forehead, wrinkles which tarnished it, a mouth tightly closed to deprive itself of bread and of outcries, and her poor blue eyes too large, with watery glance." Pauline was destined, however, to outlive her husband by many years; she died in 1946, encompassed by the filial tenderness of her son, as described in his novel *Mort d'un personnage*. Some years later, when Giono learned of Gide's death agony, his thought went back to his mother's death: "I have seen many death agonies, particularly that of my mother, made rhythmic by the slackening of her peaceful breathing. I recall what nobility she had, descending step by step into death, up to the moment when from this side I could no longer hear her."

IV *The Paternal Grandfather*

On the paternal side, Giono's ancestors were more colorful and are more important to his development as a writer. When, in the opening pages of *Angélo*, the French custom-house officer at the frontier on Mont Genèvre saw riding up "a horseman who seemed like a sheaf of gold on a black horse," we are introduced for the first time to Giono's Italian grandfather, Jean-Baptiste Giono, as he enters France as a fugitive from a death sentence rendered by the Court of Turin. From early youth Giono has been fascinated by this enigmatic, mysterious figure. At the age of seventeen he used to climb to the third floor of the dark, dilapidated house to his father's workroom—the little lamp shaking in his hand because he was trembling like a leaf—to hear his father spin fantastic tales about this Piedmontese ancestor: "It was there that the old carbonaro came to life; my father had composed for my benefit an enormous spoken novel about him, enlarged each evening with new episodes full of romantic details. This was my sugar candy."

Born exactly one hundred years before his grandson, in March,

1795, in the little town of Ivre near Turin, Jean-Baptiste was a giant who liked to enhance the effect of his six feet, six inches by enveloping his neck with a cravat tied in several knots and by wearing a stove-pipe hat, which he enjoyed having knocked off as he entered a door. Around 1832, Mazzini, banished from Piedmont for revolutionary activities, became the patron saint of Jean-Baptiste Giono who—as we read in Giono's *Voyage en Italie*—in his role as carbonaro "cut several throats very nicely in the vicinity of Pignerol in honor of the outlaw and according to prearranged plans." Jean-Baptiste then joined the troops charged with repressing the revolt of clerical peasants in Calabria, a grim and merciless repression costing many lives, which gained for him the rank of colonel. After this episode he seems to have conspired against the government of Charles Albert by forming Jacobin Clubs in favor of a republic; for this crime he was sentenced to death by default and forced to go into hiding in the chestnut-covered mountains of his estate at Montezemollo near Mondovi. Here he escaped by disfiguring himself with a scar, putting on his uniform, and passing himself off for the very officer charged with his pursuit. Arriving at Briançon, he sold his sword (once shown to Giono by the descendant of the man who bought it) and came to Aix-en-Provence where he met an old comrade, François Zola, a fugitive from justice like himself, the father of Emile Zola, and a native of Trentino.

In humanitarian zeal the two friends embarked for Algiers in order to nurse the victims of the great cholera epidemic which had broken out there. That Jean-Baptiste's service was appreciated by the authorities is amply proved by the original of a document which Giono has in his possession and which reads in translation as follows:

Algiers Square
Military Hospital of Instruction of the Dey.

The accounting officer director of the aforesaid military Hospital, the under-signed certifies that one Giono, Jean-Baptiste, substitute hospital attendant-major, has been employed to take care of the epidemic from 17 September 1835 to the first of May, 1836; that no complaint has arisen in regard to him and that his discharge is motivated only by the decrease in number of patients and at his request.

In testimony of which I have delivered to him this letter to use in case of need.

Done at the Dey, 9 March 1836,   Drioval

After the two friends returned to Aix, François Zola was given the contract for digging the canal from Aix to Marseille; he entrusted the supervision of the work to Jean-Baptiste. Jean-Baptiste married and at his death in 1845 left one son, Jean-Antoine, born two years before. The circumstances of Jean-Baptiste's death are somewhat mysterious, though there seems no doubt that he perished in the fire which consumed the offices of the construction company in the hamlet of the Frères-Gris, not far from Aix. Villeneuve[1] gives credence to the story that Jean-Baptiste committed suicide after having lost in gambling all the payroll money. However, Giono, in his *Noé*, has given a slightly more charitable version: "He went back of his own free will into a house in flames, in order to save I know not what, but certainly not a human life; he felt too much scorn for his contemporaries." Perhaps this explanation may have seemed a little cynical and unfilial to Giono, for last summer he gave me still another dénouement: Jean-Baptiste was trying to save the company's account-books from destruction. Wherever the truth may lie, this final version with its mixture of irony and heroism would seem to make a fitting conclusion to so stirring and quixotic a life.

The reader is slightly aghast at the hilarious manner which Giono is wont to employ in referring to his grandfather, one in startling contrast to the tenderness and respect he has for his parents. Thus we read in *Le Voyage:* "I have always been fond of that unscrupulous rascal. He had only one virtue and even that was of '48 vintage: he believed in the happiness of the common people through liberty. It is certainly from him that I inherit my naïve principles." Contrasting his two grandfathers who fought in Italy, Giono even went so far as to say that Jean-Baptiste "was no lover of bayonet charges. He got rid of all his enemies in the shadow and certainly from behind." On still another occasion Giono has called his grandfather, the carbonaro, "a tough buccaneer; he did some queer things in his life, and sometimes gratuitously. At times that has its effect on me."

Among the stories about his grandfather which Jean's father used to tell him was the fact that all Giono descendants were entitled to food and lodging for three days a year at the home of the priest in Montezemollo. During his trip to Italy in August, 1952, Giono stopped at the little town and learned the origin of this favor. When Jean-Baptiste was condemned to death, he had given some of his lands to the parish, in return for which the parishioners, to show their gratitude, had granted his descendants the right to be received three days a year under the priest's roof. It may not be without interest to add that, after eighty years of sequestration, Jean-Baptiste's estate was finally liquidated in 1903 for nine thousand francs, a third going to Giono's father and a third to each of his father's sisters.

V *Giono's Father*

Giono's father, Jean-Antoine, was born in Saint-Chamas in 1843. After the death of his carbonaro father, he and his two sisters were reared by their mother who supported them working as an innkeeper on the road from Marseilles to the Alps. Learning the shoemaker's trade, he set up business in a little shop in Marseilles. After the marriage of his sisters and his mother's death, Jean-Antoine was seized with a desire to revisit the land of his father's exploits. On foot, carrying his cobbler's tools, he set out for Piedmont, making a pilgrimage also to Mozart's birthplace in Salzburg. Whenever his funds gave out, he replenished them by working for a time at his trade. Like his father, he returned to France by way of Briançon and the valley of the Durance. Stopping in Manosque, he set up shop there permanently; in 1892, he married Pauline Pourcin, eleven years his junior.

One of Giono's most appealing traits is the respect he has always shown for the humble trade of his father and mother. He has sometimes grouped himself with three other contemporary writers—Jean Guéhenno, Louis Guilloux, and Lucien Jacques, who likewise were shoemaker's sons—as forming with him the brotherhood of cobblers in literature today. His father occupies an important role in many of Giono's writings, and his presence overshadows all others in the autobiographic *Jean le bleu.* "I remember my father's workroom. I can never pass by a shoemaker's shop without thinking that my father still exists, somewhere beyond this world, sitting at a spirit table, with his blue apron, his shoemaker's knife, his wax-ends, his awls, making shoes of angel leather for some thousand-legged god."

Though Jean-Antoine loved his craft, his true vocation was that of a healer of wounds, both physical and spiritual. Old people made a procession to his room to have him bathe their eczema with sedative water, and the whole place reeked with camphor. Epileptics called upon him for special ministrations of tenderness. While Giono's mother made shrugs and grimaces of despair behind the cupboard door, Jean-Antoine welcomed with open arms revolutionaries from Italy, anarchists from France, or fugitives of any sort in trouble and needing shelter: "I do not know by what miracle they came. It must have been transmitted to them, like the language of the swallows, or perhaps marked in some corner of the inn, carved with a knife in the wall. Some sign, a circle, some crosses, a star, a sun, a mark that must have said in their wretched language: 'Go to Père Jean's.'" As Giono was to write later, he inherited from his father that "look which attracted lost dogs."

A disciple of Fourier and Blanqui, Jean-Antoine hated social injustice and was quite capable on occasion of writing letters of protest to the Pope or to the King of Italy. Inheriting his father's passionate desire for liberty, he did not, however, share the carbonaro's penchant for violence. Though he was ever willing to harbor outlaws at some danger to himself and at a cost he could ill afford, he endeavored to calm and restrain them rather than to accede to their plans for revolutionary activity. When, for instance, a French anarchist escaped to Switzerland after having hidden for a fortnight in the cobbler's home and after explaining his project for fomenting an uprising, Jean-Antoine shook his head reproachfully, "That will cause bloodshed. I'd rather be a healer. You must put me where I can heal."

In the drawer of his desk, Giono's father kept side by side the Bible and a portrait of Voltaire. Several critics have professed to find in him a tendency towards Protestantism, yet he felt that "religion no longer has any connection with God." In the story "La Ville des hirondelles" Giono states categorically that, contrary to certain statements of critics, neither he nor his father was a Protestant. Although they often read together the Bible and the treatises of St. Thomas Aquinas on God and on human nature, these texts were treasured primarily for their poetic content: "It was truly beautiful poetry, very beautiful wisdom of very great strength. They were beautiful books."

Besides his respect for the craftmanship of the artisan, Giono owes also to his father his sensuous enjoyment of nature. Isolated in the dark loneliness of his third-floor workshop, Jean-Antoine felt a desperate longing for a garden, a desire which "blazed in our midst like a fire." Finally he succeeded in renting a little plot of ground on the outskirts of the town, ten meters of terrace fertilized by detritus and dirty water; there he cultivated rose bushes and hyssop. After the noon-day meal he would carry off a chair on his shoulder and sit between his two rose bushes, while the pigeons from the convent came to perch on his shoulder. Then he would say to his little son, "If when you get to be a man you know these two things, poetry and the science of extinguishing wounds, then you *will* be a man." Later Jean-Antoine was able to buy for a hundred and fifty francs a tiny plot of hillside land with a few olive trees. Here he had a brick hut built and a well dug beneath the trees. Jean Giono would go there furtively to hide behind the honeysuckle to watch his father feed his rabbits: "It was there [his father] developed the habit of humming with mouth closed, a dull sound, devoid of color or form, monotonous, restrained, strangely magnetic, as haunting as the beat of a distant drum."

Though largely self-tutored, Jean-Antoine seems to have written several poems, including one in Lamartinian style about the birth of his son. It would be impossible, I think, to exaggerate the influence of the father's philosophy of life, with its blend of mysticism and simple realism, on his son. When news came of the first successful flight of the Wright brothers, Francesc Odripano (a poetic character modeled on Giono's father) was quite unimpressed; his shrewd comment may not be without application to our Gagarins, Shepards, and Titovs of the present day: "It won't change anything. Because the whole happiness of man is in the little valleys. As long as we invent and progress in mechanical things and not in love, we shall not achieve happiness." Jean-Antoine was fond of saying, "Most of one's time is spent with oneself. One must try to make it always agreeable company." Yet, as Giono wrote many years later in *Triomphe de la vie*, his father had time to plant four chestnut trees, two lindens, twenty cherry trees, and a hundred vines (in addition to making beautiful shoes) and "he had likewise time to love, to suffer and to die."

CHAPTER 2

Giono's Childhood and Youth

I *The House*

JEAN-ANTOINE was fifty years old when his son was born on
March 30, 1895, in the old street with the poetic appellation
Sans Nom. Shortly afterward the family moved to the vast but
dilapidated dwelling on 14 Grand' Rue that was rented from Mlle
Delphine Pieirisnard. For the student of Giono's writings it is instructive to compare the realistic and exact description of this
house given in *Les Pages immortelles de Virgile* with the romantic
and idealized transcription which we find in *Jean le bleu.* The
entire second floor was uninhabitable; the ceilings and floors were
rotted out and the old beams creaked day and night behind never-
opened doors, a paradise for rats and spiders. Though the rain
seeped through to all the floors, the third housed the cobbler shop
of his father, and the ground floor was the laundry of his mother
and her three washerwomen—"a huge table with a white cloth.
My mother would sing like a bird, the others joining in." Back of
the laundry was the bedroom the whole family shared and the
dark kitchen. Giono's bed was in the corner least exposed to the
infiltration from the gutters, but on stormy nights his father often
pushed the bed from place to place and tried to catch the drips in
basins or buckets. As for his parents, after several vain efforts to
find a dry refuge, they would finally go to sleep with their heads
sheltered by large umbrellas.

As young Jean grew up, however, this monstrous dwelling took
on an aura of poetic mystery and beauty. He loved the vast attic
above his father's workroom, "sonorous as a ship." In the atmosphere of the lower stories also one could not keep from dreaming
—"too much decay on the walls, too much darkness that smelled
of mushrooms, too many sounds in the thick walls." The little boy
was especially fascinated by a gray shadow on the north wall,
which was crossed sometimes by the pale flash of a rat. As his
gaze entered more and more deeply into this shadow, he was

finally able to see "the lady" who formed the focal point of his dreams: "Her face was oval and slightly rounded. She was green but the greenest part was in her eyes and all the color of her skin could be only a reflection, the luminous glow of her gaze. At the place where her mouth was, the disease of the wall had eaten to the bricks and it was blood-red like real flesh."

The inner courtyard also, into which sunlight penetrated only briefly at noon, with its abandoned well and its teeming flock of sheep waiting to be led to the slaughterhouse, was full of fascination for the young lad.

II *His First School*

Soon the time came for a decision concerning Jean's schooling. On the one hand, there was the municipal *collège* of Manosque, a shabby little institution banished by the town beyond the walls towards the hills; on the other hand, the aristocratic school of the Sisters of the Presentation, surrounded by lilacs and giant box-wood, was "sustained morally, pecuniarily and beatifically by everybody that walked in silk in the town." Because of the agnostic views of his father, as well as the cost of twenty sous a week, it may seem surprising that the religious school was chosen. One day an elegantly attired lady had come to Jean-Antoine's workroom, haughtily seated herself on the edge of a chair, and implored him to send Jean, "the fine delicate child who looks so much like his mother," to the Sisters' school where he would receive so much individual instruction and be kept until six in the evening. She reminded Jean's father that Pauline had been a member of their congregation and that, because of this fact, the repairing of shoes for the Sisters had been given to him. She knew that Jean-Antoine was a good man in spite of everything, for he allowed Pauline to go to mass. "Pauline is free," my father answered. "If Jean is of my blood, he will make the right decision. Send him if it gives you any pleasure."

One of the three girls employed by Jean's mother usually accompanied the little boy to school. Despite the flattering epithets of the lady of the visitation, Giono insists that at this time he was far from having a "fine" appearance because of his "long, thin, unattractive face, redeemed only by tender eyes." Yet his mother had done everything possible to make him presentable: "In what a majestic starched collar were my shoulders encased, and by how many hands was the magnificent sky blue silk of my tie puffed and bowed."

On Easter Monday at vespers there was to be an impressive ceremony at the school to which all the mothers in their silk and finery had been invited. Little Jean was to have the honor of reciting the homage to the Virgin, a sandstone statue which Jean had heard singing in the wind where she dwelt in the midst of the flowering almond orchard. But on that day, either because no wind was blowing or because she was intimidated by the presence of so many fashionable people, the Virgin was silent. "Begin, my child," said the Mother Superior. Raising his eyes to the Virgin, Jean addressed her: "Good Mother, you who are the fair open pomegranate and the ripe orange." Then he suddenly burst into sobs. "She is dead, she is dead," he cried. When everyone rushed forward in consternation, little Jean made his escape after catching a glimpse of his mother, "to whom the matter was being rather coldly explained." The scandal caused by this unfortunate occurrence seems to have been irrevocable, for Jean, now six, began to attend the municipal school where he remained ten years.

III Relations with Father

From the time little Jean was able to climb the long stairway alone, his most enjoyable hours were spent at his father's side in the workshop. Sometimes on returning from school he would find his father struggling desperately with some almost impossible job. At such moments the old cobbler would lay down his work, fill a pipe, say "Well now, sonny," and then ask his son to tell him all about his school work and games. When this subject was exhausted, he would begin to spin tales concerning his own father, the carbonaro colonel. Next morning at dawn the father would creep up to his shop, and soon Jean would hear him humming triumphantly: he had solved the difficult problem. As the little boy in his nightshirt entered the workroom and saw his father's patient, skilled hands moving over the leather like birds constructing a nest, he had never felt "so much hope in living, so much certainty concerning the beauty of being in the world." He realized now that, "thanks to my love for him, I saw my father in his eternal strength." He would reclose the door; soon he would hear the clock strike seven and his father descend for his morning coffee.

On some occasions Jean-Antoine took his son for a trip to Marseilles. An essential feature of these journeys, which seem to have impressed Giono deeply, since he has described them twice, both in *Noé* and *Voyage en Italie*, was a visit to a pond in Marseilles with the somewhat rhetorical title, Le Tour du Monde. For the price of two sous each, ten children were rowed slowly around the pond in a boat which had the form of a steamer. Giono was heartbroken to leave his father on land, and Jean-Antoine, equally distressed at the separation, would follow the boat around the pond as it made "its trip around the world."

IV *Nature and the Classics*

One of Jean-Antoine's good friends was the "baile" or master-shepherd, Massot from Corbières, who always came for a visit with him on days of the Manosque fair. In 1906, when the little Jean was eleven years old, his father decided that it would be good for his health, as well as for his better understanding of the world of nature, to send him for a few months to live with Massot and his wife, who loved children dearly but had none of their own. One day, therefore, the shoemaker got a light cart, installed a small trunk, and drove with Jean to Massot's home in Corbières, named after the *corbeaux* or crows which flew about it in such numbers.

In the meantime a mysterious stranger, to whom Jean-Antoine had once loaned money in a time of distress, brought the cobbler a package of books—an *Odyssey*, a Hesiod, a little Virgil in two volumes, and a Bible bound in black—in partial payment of his debt. Every week Massot brought the boy back to Manosque for a lesson with the stranger. The time came, however, when Massot was no longer able to make the weekly journey; and Jean-Antoine therefore sent the dark, mysterious stranger to live with the Massots in Corbières. Accompanied by a shepherd dog, the two led their sheep to pasture early in the morning; there the stranger read aloud in his deep musical voice from the book brought along with their lunch of bread and cheese. It was thus that Giono made his first acquaintance with the classics: "I read the *Iliad* amidst the ripened wheat. It was within me that Achilles stamped back and forth in his tent, with the wrath of his heavy tread. It was within me that Patroclus bled. It was within me that the wind of the sea broke over the prows." When his father came for him in the fall to take him back to school, he found Jean in such robust health that he repeated the experiment the following year.

V *The Bank*

Giono's scholastic record was excellent, and he received a scholarship to prepare himself for the diploma in science-languages. He received honors for his essay on the battle of Pavia (a subject he has recently developed into a book). Latin was not offered in the little *collège*, but some old notebooks of grades which can still be found in the school library show that he was excellent in English, good in practical exercises and other subjects; but, ironically enough, he was barely average in French composition. One is reminded of the fact that Giono's contemporary, Antoine de Saint-Exupéry, likewise a great poetic stylist in prose, failed his examination in French but was excellent in mathematics.

Jean-Antoine was now growing old and feeble. When his apprentice Pancrace left him to set up shop for himself, he had not replaced him and had worked alone in the cold, dark room. Business had slackened because of factory competition, and the cobbler was now earning only thirty to forty francs a week—and only twenty to twenty-five in the off-season, a sum which Pauline equaled with her laundry. One evening Giono heard his father get up in the night and fall heavily to the floor. It was only a slight attack, but it was enough to make his son realize for the first time that his father was using his last remnant of strength to keep the family alive. Next afternoon in school, when the lamps were being lit for study hall, Jean felt such uneasiness concerning his father that he asked permission to leave, ran all the way home, rushed through the laundry, climbed the stairs four steps at a time, and dropped down at his father's side. The father understood his son's solicitude; as he gently stroked Jean's hair, he murmured, "No, my son, not yet." Nevertheless, for his own peace of mind, Jean insisted on dropping out of school, less than a year away from graduation, in order to take a job. His own desire was to become a shoemaker, but his father was adamant—"the only time this admirable man's love made a mistake"—and instead a place was found in October, 1911, for Jean as *chasseur* or messenger at the Manosque branch of the Comptoir National d'Escomptes. On the last day of November Jean was able to place proudly on the evening table two gold pieces of twenty and of ten francs. "The house in which the rain entered was saved."

At first his work consisted in placing letters in envelopes and carrying them to the old houses in Manosque to which they were addressed. Before long, however, he was entrusted with the more prosaic task of adding up columns of thirty-five figures. A slight geographical interest relieved the tedium of these figures, for it was necessary to write in the second column the place name where payment was to be made. Jean's ardent imagination made it possible for him to see from time to time in a flash "the green shoulder of a hill, the wind of a plateau on which night was falling on a chestnut grove." Then he came to realize also that the writing of figures could become an artistic exercise in drawing. Another part of his functions was to hold open the door and to bow politely at the entrance of wealthy customers whose accounts were listed with at least five zeroes.

To withstand the tedium associated with these duties, Jean divided himself into two distinct personalities: "There were twenty or thirty little wheels in my head to which I had given the task of understanding dignified politeness and beautiful penmanship," he states amusingly in *Jean le bleu.* "All that part of the mechanism was called 'come here' and it earned thirty francs a month, and that bought the potatoes. The greater part nothing could touch. It was called 'Blue Boy.' They would have loved to catch it and shut it up in the livery that bowed to the ladies; but it was too late."

On Sundays the little town was silent until vespers rang out at three in the afternoon. Then Manosque suddenly divided itself into two factions. One part, dressed in sober black, with gloves and muff tripped lightly to church, carrying foot-warmers. A more motley array in red, blue, green, scarlet, and saffron hastened to the ball at the Casino. Giono was often sorely tempted to join this boisterous group, but he thought the buffets he might receive there would ill befit his position of respectability as a banker. Besides, there was always the question of finances. Every Sunday he was allotted from his salary the sum of two francs—just enough to order two of the Garnier collection of classics and have two sous left over to post a letter to Garnier in Paris. Though he knew it would take a week to receive an answer, he soon became anxious and then full of despair until one morning the postman told him he had a package: "Joy and joyous tears. Thus on 20 December 1911 I received Virgil." Since the pleasure Giono felt with his new acquisition was at first physical, he carried it around for several days in his pocket, postponing the first reading until he could take it with him to the edge of the woods during Christmas vacation.

VI *Experiences as Soldier*

Giono's recital of his boyhood in *Jean le bleu* ends with his call to the colors in early autumn, 1914. After his romantic childhood, a new chapter opened in his life; his five years of military service were to mark his soul with an ineffaceable scar and bring forth the passionate pacifism that becomes one of the leitmotivs of his later career: "Beyond this book there is a deep wound from which all men of my age are suffering." In the light of this effect, Professor Peyre has affirmed: *"Jean le bleu* receives its full significance from the last chapter on the tragic massacre that buried the rosy dreams of his adolescence." [1]

Yet Giono, like many another lad, left for the adventure with light-hearted gaiety: "It was easy for me to set out for the war without any great feeling of emotion, simply because I was young, and over all young men they were blowing a wind that sang of pirates and the ocean sail." Nor did he look back on his training days on the Champ de Mars at Briançon without a trace of nostalgia. Attached to the 159th Alpine Infantry, he did guard duty in February, 1915, for a month before leaving for the front. In clear weather, as he relates in *Voyage en Italie,* he could see towards the east a yellow fog which was Piedmont. When an old sergeant insisted that they could even glimpse the smoke from Turin, Giono was reminded of his father and of the stories he used to tell about the colonel. It was in the barracks of Briançon Castle, Giono recalled, and more particularly in the recess of a certain window on the third floor that he "took pleasure in not possessing, in being deprived of even essential things such as liberty and even the liberty to live." He can still remember scratching this sentiment in the stone with the point of his knife.

When he was granted leave to visit his parents before leaving for the front, his old father, with tears streaming down his white beard on to his leather apron, embraced him in the workshop. For four years Giono saw service, first in the 159th Alpine regiment and then in the 140th from Grenoble. Reminiscences of these war years are to be found in many of Giono's books. In *Refus d'obéissance* Giono enumerates his campaigns: Eparges, Verdun, Vaux, Noyon, Saint-Quentin, Chemin des Dames, Vinon-Chevrillon, and Mount Kemmel—names which evoke memories from readers old enough to re-live those stirring days. Of the men in his sixth company, the only other survivors at the end of the war were Captain Vidon and Private Martin. And no wonder, for the sixth company was a little receptacle for the 27th division: "When the bushel was empty of men, when there were only a few remaining at the bottom, like grains stuck in the grooves, they would fill it up again with fresh men."

In his Preface to the *Carnets de moleskine* of his friend Lucien Jacques, Giono has given a harrowing picture of his experiences during the battle of Fort Vaux at Verdun. For an entire week the men from the commissary department bringing provisions failed to arrive since they were all killed on the way. Hungry and thirsty, the soldiers first seized the water cans and the bread of the corpses. When this resource was exhausted, and after four days without liquid, Giono and his companions licked up rainwater from the ground, swallowed pellets of earth, and even ate a raw rat to stifle the craving of their empty stomachs. There were nine men compressed in a hole barely adequate for three—that is, until the man nearest the opening was killed. After that, his dead body served in some measure to protect the remaining eight from shell fragments. After being relieved, Giono was sent for a time as artillery observer to the fort of La Pompelle, occupied by a Russian garrison. In one of his short stories in the volume *Solitude de la pitié*, Giono gives a moving account of the friendship which sprang up between him and a Russian giant, Ivan Ivanovitch Kossiakoff, with whom he would signal to the batteries the appearance of enemy convoys on the road. Once Ivan saw a German officer cutting hay for his horse in a field just before dusk, but Ivan was persuaded by Giono's ardent entreaty not to give the signal to fire.

VII *Pacifism*

When Giono returned home on leave in the spring of 1916, he found his father already talking of the approach of death which he did not fear. To the reproach of Pauline that he was letting his imagination run away with him, the old shoemaker replied that he had never used his imagination to represent sure and certain things, but only for all the rest: "Towards me he raised his gray eyes in which a fleeting distress was trembling like water rippled by the wind: 'When I need to imagine,' he said, 'it is in silence.'"

On this visit Giono's mother broke the news to him of the death at the front of his dearest friend, Louis David. "If you had only died for honorable things; if you had fought for love or in getting food for your little ones. But no. First they deceived you and then they killed you in the war." In the poignant anguish of these words in the last chapter of *Jean le bleu* we see the beginning of Giono's ardent pacifism; it was caused by his conviction of the utter uselessness of war: "You are a shadow there behind my chair. I shall never touch your hand again, I shall never hear your voice again; never see your good face with its honesty and its broad smile. I know that you are there, near me, as are all the dead I have loved and who loved me. . . . But you are dead."

VIII *Last Campaigns*

In 1917 while Giono's regiment was in the muddy Santerre plain, a strange and unreasoning terror came over his unit. The rumor that a phantom covered with a German overcoat wandered over the plain and killed soldiers deeply affected the morale of Giono's company. According to Villeneuve, it was then that Captain Vidon requested Giono to tell stories to the soldiers during the evening hour when panic gripped them most. Giono related tales from *Les Misérables*, elaborating on the episodes which seemed to captivate them, such as that of Bishop Myriel pardoning Jean Valjean for his theft of the candlesticks or that of the rescue of little Cosette from the rapacious Thénardiers.

The last two years of the war were the most terrible for Giono because of the slaughter of Nivelle's bloody attack at the Chemin des Dames and later the fighting around Saint-Quentin and Mount Kemmel. In his preface to Jean Guéhenno's *Journal d'un homme de 40 ans*, Giono states that it was in the Vinon-Chevrillon sector that he suffered most: "That spot of earth was my cross. I bled with my feet, my hands, my forehead and my heart."

As Giono tells us in *Refus d'obéissance*, he received no French war decoration nor was he ever promoted from his rank of second-class private—possibly because, in order not to kill anyone, he always mounted to the attack without a gun, or with one which he had rendered harmless. His only wound was a slight burn on his eyelids from gas in May, 1918, after the attack on Mount Kemmel, for which he was given treatment in a hospital in Woordmouth, England. Though Giono insists that he was always overcome with fear in the trenches, he helped a British officer, blinded by this same gas, to escape from the burning hospital and was decorated by the British government for his act of courage. Finally, almost five years after induction, Giono was demobilized in October, 1919.

CHAPTER 3

Lucien Jacques and Giono's Début in Literature

I Post-War Career

WHEN Giono returned from the war, he was transferred from the Manosque to the Marseilles office of the Bureau National d'Escompte. In the train with him he carried, according to Chonez,[1] a copy of *The Jungle Book* by Rudyard Kipling. Giono was struck by the phrase "It was seven o'clock of a very warm evening on the hills of Senoe"; and this simple phrase, he told Chonez, fired his ambition to become a writer: "I felt with certainty that I too was capable of writing." So, in the basement of the bank in Marseilles, he began to write his first eclogues and poems in prose, some of which were published in the Marseilles magazine known as *La Criée*.

In 1920 Giono received permission to return to the Manosque branch of the bank where he remained for almost ten years. In *Voyage en Italie* he recalls this period without bitterness and even with pleasure, in spite of his timid awe for the inspector who verified his work and on whom his whole future depended: "He was a stout, bearded man who smoked cigars and did not hide his scorn for the vague expression which my blue eyes gave me. Though I was an excellent employee, as he admitted, he kept me constantly dancing on a tight rope." Yet Giono considered it a valuable experience to have his career exposed to danger from the very beginning; and, when in 1934 this inspector requested Giono to inscribe one of his books, he did so very effusively. But, writes Giono, "He continued to terrify me. I understood that he was embarrassed in his needs, incapable of being very good or very bad, just like everybody else." This apprehension of the young Giono with so many mouths to feed is shown also by the fact that, after his weekend rambles in the hills, he would return Sunday evenings to make quite sure that the building housing the bank had not disappeared.

[38]

For some time Jean-Antoine had been growing more and more infirm. He had become very emaciated; "his hand as it left the door knob floated a moment, imponderable in the air. His eyes looked through things as he took several soft swaying steps as if he were walking on a cloud. His thin mouth was gnawed by a kind of acrid fever and was nothing but a trickle of vinegar under his mustache." Though he did not complain of the pain from his liver, his character had changed; he had become cruel and hard. On one of his last walks with his son, he had talked of God as an idea of human invention; and he had said, "The terrible thing is to suffer alone." In the light of Giono's disillusionment later with the failure of his humanitarian hopes and their cruel rejection in World War II, the words of his father seem strangely prophetic: "Where I made a mistake, was when I wanted to be good and helpful. You will make a mistake like me." Then his father began to puff on his pipe and to hum "that monotonous tune that enveloped him like the silk of a cocoon."

In April, 1920, Jean-Antoine died: "He was lying in the back of his bed, quite changed, shrivelled and shrunk by a terrible suffering." His father's portrait, as well as his memory, was never to leave Giono who loved his parent so much "not only because he was my father but because he was what he was. I admired him; I still do."

In June of the same year Giono married his fiancée, Elise Maurin. Of this union were born two daughters: Aline, in 1924; Sylvie, in 1932.

II *First Publications*

Giono did not know Greece except from his readings in translation from Virgil, Hesiod, Theocritus, and Homer. Yet, as he tells us in his Preface to the recent de luxe edition of *Accompagnés de la flûte,* he had such need of Greece that he invented it: "I had at my disposition orchards of olive trees and land cut by deep valleys. My imagination had no difficulty to exaggerate in spiritual values the bronze of the orchards, the roundness of the sky and the distant mountains. I spent all my Sundays in Delphi." Since the requirements of his work in the bank forced Giono to remain shut up between four walls, it was necessary for his imagination to break down these walls and to give his fancy free rein. Giono was at liberty not only on Sundays but also on Monday mornings.

The latter he employed in long walks through the olive groves: "These groves led me to books; these books led me to write."

He wrote in the fields on whatever paper he happened to have with him—on the back of old envelopes, even on cigarette paper. It was partly these Monday mornings which determined Giono's choice of readings, but even more it was his impecunious condition. Of the 250 franc salary which supported his wife, his mother, and an uncle who lived with them, he had allotted himself five francs a month for the purchase of books. Whereas modern authors such as Anatole France cost 7.50 francs, he could buy the classics—Homer, Sophocles, Aeschylus, Euripides, Virgil, Aristophanes, and Cervantes—for ninety-five centimes.

At this time (1922) his friendship for Lucien Jacques began, one which was destined to have an unlimited influence on his life and which was to continue without interruption until Jacques's death in 1961. After Giono had sent a poem to *La Criée* (the Marseilles magazine) and a few days after its publication, he had received an enthusiastic letter signed Lucien Jacques, who seemed to have taken Giono for a sailor. He was not entirely mistaken, for, as Giono says, "I was in fact a mariner on this imaginary sea with the purple depths of the mountains barring my horizon." In any case, Giono answered immediately and thus began a correspondence of which Giono's part is published in the recent reissue of *Accompagnés de la flûte*. Then the time arrived when correspondence was no longer necessary, for Lucien Jacques came from his home at Cyprès Saint-Jean near Grasse to visit the Gionos; in fact, he became almost a member of the family and accompanied them on many summer holiday trips to the mountains.

Besides the "Chroniques de l'Artisan" which Jacques wrote for *La Criée*, he had begun a collection of brochures, *Les Cahiers de l'Artisan*, in which he printed at his own expense texts which appealed to him. This work was purely a labor of love, for these *Cahiers* brought him no financial return; his modest livelihood came from the painting of *aquarelles*. So impressed was Jacques with Giono's literary promise that he at once offered to publish something by him in one of the *Cahiers*. Though the circulation of the *Cahiers* did not exceed one hundred and fifty copies, Giono, immensely gratified, proceeded to write a group of prose poems, on classic and Provençal themes, that were full of charming bucolic images expressed in rhythmic melodious prose. The first part entitled "Dans la parole de Virgile" was inspired by phrases from the *Aeneid;* the second part, "Vers les bosquets d'Akadé-mos," by sentences taken from Plato. The title for the collection was *Accompagnés de la flûte.*

The immediate success of this publication was somewhat less than earth-shaking, despite a favorable review in *Mercure de France,* for only five or six copies were sold. Giono would have been consoled, however, if he had recalled that Stendhal, whom he later came to admire so passionately, had sold in ten years only eleven copies of his treatise *De l'Amour.* Strangely enough, however, all the copies of *Accompagnés,* even the one belonging to Giono, had disappeared from circulation twenty-five years later when the de luxe edition of *Accompagnés de la flûte,* with exquis-ite illustrations by Lucien Jacques, was reissued in 1959. Far more important than the material success of this first little volume was the intimate association begun with Lucien Jacques, for it gained for Giono a perceptive and encouraging critic and an acquaint-ance with a group of young writers and artists outside his Ma-nosque circle.

III *Character of Lucien Jacques*

Lucien Jacques, a native of Varennes in the Argonne region of northern France, like Giono was a veteran of World War I. Many years later, in 1939, he recounted this tragic experience in *Carnets de moleskine,* for which Giono wrote the preface already mentioned. Like his friend, Jacques had become so shaken in morale by his seven years of military service, by the loss of so many dear friends, and by the sight of so many corpses that he had fallen into a state of bitter pessimism from which he emerged only by publishing a volume of poems. Unable to adjust himself to life in Paris where he stayed after the war, he came to Provence which he loved for its great spaciousness. At his home near Grasse he became a friend of H. G. Wells, who persuaded him to trans-late a book of Sassoon into French. He was also a great friend of the American dancer, Isadora Duncan; and he designed the fron-tispiece for an American book about her. When I met Jacques in the summer of 1960, he was living in a picturesque studio, for-merly an old mill, in the little town of Gréoux-les-Bains, some ten miles from Manosque. He commuted often to his lovely home of Montjustin when he could find a friend to drive him; for, like

Giono, Lucien Jacques was strangely unskilled in mechanical matters and was unable to drive a car.

In appearance and personality Lucien Jacques was as unlike Giono as could be imagined. Frail and slender of body, gentle and almost timid in expression, he possessed an indescribable, wistful charm which was enhanced by his almost excessive modesty. "I am not a man of action like Giono," he said. What drew the two friends together, aside from their common abhorrence of war, was the fact that both were sons of shoemakers; moreover, both were "free men, capable of writing letters to the Pope about injustice, both of them poets in Lamartinian and Hugonian style." Yet, when Jacques was asked why he did not write a book on Giono, he replied that he had no desire to be an Eckermann for a Goethe; and, after all, he had his own life to lead: "I would either have to eulogize or judge my friend and I do not wish to do either." Despite his unpretentiousness, Lucien Jacques was a creative artist in many fields—printing, engraving, painting, translation, poetry, and autobiography as demonstrated by his journal of war days referred to above. Later mention will be made of his collaboration with Giono in several works, the last being his beautiful illustrations for the de luxe edition of *Crésus* in 1960. He was equally at home in the world of art and in that of literature, and his paintings were shown in many exhibitions in Paris, Marseilles, and Nice. One of these watercolors, composed in Giono's kitchen as Jacques looked over the roofs of Manosque, was the inspiration for the famous episode on the roof tops in Giono's novel *Le Hussard sur le toit*. Lucien Jacques died at Easter time in 1961.

IV   *Greek Influence*

Contemporary French drama shows many examples of Greek influence. To mention only a few, there are the *Antigone* of Anouilh; Cocteau's *Antigone, Orphée,* and *La Machine Infernale;* Giraudoux' *Amphytrion 38, Electre,* and *La Guerre de Troie n'aura pas lieu* (*Tiger at the Gates*); *Les Mouches* of Sartre; and the *Oedipe* of André Gide. Understandably, however, the influence of Greek mythology and literature has been less evident on the contemporary French novel; and, if we except the philosophic tales of Gide, Jean Giono is perhaps the only important contemporary novelist to follow this tendency.

At the same time Giono was composing *Accompagnés de la*

flûte, he was writing from the age of twenty-five to thirty his first novel, *Naissance de l'Odyssée.* As he himself declared in an interview published March 13, 1937, in *Les Nouvelles Littéraires,* he had begun to devour the Garnier classics, which he had chosen for reasons of economy: "The Greeks were revealed to my dazzled mind. I have revived, or rather I have made actual, the heroes of Homer and of Sophocles whom I found unchanged in my native province. From that day on I had found my path: to renew the great Greek tragedies." Henri Peyre has explained Giono's enthusiasm for Greek themes as due in part to the similarity between the two civilizations of ancient Greece and modern Provence: "The reading of ancient poets in translation was for the young Jean the supreme revelation. . . . Giono had not learned Greek but he grew up in a land where peasants to this day winnow their grain, pluck their olives, and milk their goats much as their Mediterranean forefathers did in the time of Ulysses or Theocritus. He felt the Classics spontaneously and lived them in his body. They gave him, according to his favorite phrase, 'a kick in the stomach.' "

According to his biographer Chonez, Giono preferred the *Odyssey* to the *Iliad.* Next in order came the Greek tragic poets and Virgil and, after these, Stendhal, Dostoievski, and Shakespeare. We should not forget, however, the Bible, which his father read to him constantly throughout his childhood. Henri Fluchère, indeed, gives the Bible equal importance with Homer: "The two antipodal great creations of the human mind in which Giono alternately refreshes his inspiration are the Bible and the *Odyssey* and we find in his works the deep moral teachings of the one and the powerful lyricism of both." At the age of twenty Giono possessed a library of a hundred volumes, a most unusual collection for his little town of Manosque.

The circumstances surrounding the inception of *Naissance de l'Odyssée,* as related by Giono to the journalist Henri Perruchot,[2] are extremely amusing. One day, when Giono was reading the *Odyssey* while walking through the hills, he happened to visit the isolated farm of a friend who, like Odysseus, was a hog raiser. When Giono left the book open on the kitchen table while he went out to the pig sty, his friend began to read the book. On his return, the friend asked him if that was his book and commented, "It's a beautiful novel." "No, it's not a novel," Giono replied; "it's the *Odyssey*." "That makes no difference," his friend answered; "it's a novel all the same, a whole lot better than those newspaper serials." Impressed by such enthusiasm, Giono left the book with his friend; and he learned later that, during the following winter, he had read the entire book aloud to the neighbors who shared the evenings with him. And the result was that he obtained voluntary workers for sorting his olives and shelling his almonds. While talking with his friend, Giono had the impression of speaking with Odysseus in person; and, little by little, he began to incorporate the Homeric episodes in the setting of Provence.

V *The Narrative*

In his article on Giono, Henri Peyre congratulates him for refraining, unlike his contemporaries, from belittling Hellenic themes with irony and facile anachronisms; we can agree with this critic's statement but still point out that irony, not belittling but genial, is the basis for Giono's entire treatment of the Odysseus theme. This irony is evident at the beginning of the narrative when Odysseus, stranded on Circe's Island, encounters a Menelaus thick and fat as a tuna fish; moreover, he is emptied of that gnawing fever which had agitated him, saber in hand, when attacking the walls of Troy. Now Menelaus has the charms of Helen all to himself; but, since his return from the war, he finds life far different from the paradise of his dreams. Much of his property has been stolen, and young men without respect have even tried to force the doors of his mistress, a little Asiatic brunette whom he had to hide in a Spartan suburb because of his fear of Helen. Unaware that Odysseus had not yet heard the news, Menelaus blurts out the scandalous affairs of Penelope, first with several young lovers and now with a certain Antinoüs who is squandering her estate. Despite the uncomfortable vision of a possible Aegisthus ready to slay him upon his return, Odysseus no longer finds delight in the favors of Circe and persuades a skipper to take him back to Greece.

After reaching the mainland, Odysseus spends his first night in a rustic inn full of peasant women whom a muleteer, poking fun at their morals, likens to the wife of Odysseus in her affair with Antinoüs. When Odysseus shouts that Antinoüs would not last long if her husband should return, a blind bard with a guitar— the only anachronism in the work—insists that Odysseus is dead.

To this Odysseus retorts that he has seen him alive only a day or two ago; then he begins to concoct fabulous stories of his exploits in order to explain his delay in returning from Troy. The blind singer, enchanted by the new material for his song, rides next day with a cart driver to Megalopolis; but Odysseus loses his way in the forest and arrives there only several days later. Taken by his host to hear some singers in the public square, he is astonished to hear his own fantastic stories which the blind bard had already transmitted to his colleagues.

Fear of the vengeance of the gods now comes over Odysseus: "he had lied, lied at a stretch, as one breathes, as one drinks when one is athirst, to such an extent that now there was nothing left in his life, his imagination crystallizing over every jot of truth a scintillating carapace of lies—Odysseus. The name no longer would indicate that fox-like nose, those thin lips, those eyes hollowed by the habit of mendacious revery with unfathomable glances, but an eccentric medley of giants, of carnal goddesses, of oceans beating upon the jagged shores of isles forlorn. And he was afraid to appear before Penelope deformed by this ingurgitation of adventures too big for him."

Now in Ithaca Penelope had heard from a bard that Odysseus was still alive, not the Odysseus she used to know, driving pigs with a stick and bending under the weight of acorn sacks, but a man so much more handsome. "I could see him," she says in the lyricism of Giono's prose. "His hands were full of archipelagos and islands. The divine surge of unknown seas flowed between his fingers. In his eyes was the azure of a hundred ports. They launched ships to balance lightly on the impalpable sea of the air."

She learns from the swineherd Eumeus that Odysseus had arrived three days ago on a fishing boat. His son Telemachus, anxious at first to help him fight Antinoüs with clubs, finally sails away in disgust because his father, now a muddy, dejected old man, kept muttering "No fight." Kalidassa, Penelope's maid who is also in love with Antinoüs, brings him a message warning him of Odysseus' return. Though Antinoüs would like nothing better than to flee and console himself with Kalidassa's charms, he is persuaded by Penelope to remain and to pretend that he is merely a friend of Telemachus.

Odysseus now appears; and Penelope, uncertain of his identity because of his age and ragged costume, places him at the foot of the table while she listens to the conversation of a swine merchant who tells fabulous stories of the deeds of Odysseus, including his escape from the Cyclops by tying his men under the bellies of sheep. But, when he relates how Odysseus had once thrown the discus farther than anyone from a standing position and without removing his scarf, the athletic Antinoüs protests this assertion vigorously. At this moment the old beggar Odysseus, intoxicated not only by the wine he has drunk but also by the recital of his own story, contradicts Antinoüs sharply. The merchant, delighted by this unexpected support, urges the beggar to attack; and, when he hesitates, he gives him such a push that his fist strikes the chin of Antinoüs. Odysseus closes his eyes in horror while awaiting the return blow; but, when he finally opens them, he sees Antinoüs running in panic through the orchard.

As Antinoüs crosses a marsh, his feet are caught by a creeper which he takes for a hostile god; but he finally reaches safety on a lofty cliff from which he plans to slide down to his boat and escape. Suddenly, however, the soil gives way, carrying with it in the landslide Antinoüs and three pine trees. When Odysseus arrives, he sees the lifeless body of his rival floating in the water below: "Evening was about to fall. The gentle breeze brought with it more fresh and joyous the pearly notes of the distant flute. The air was filled with the delightful perfume of an acacia. It was good to be alive. Odysseus gulped greedily two big draughts of this melodious wind, repeating in a low voice: 'Antinoüs.'"

On his return Penelope is awaiting him tenderly, anxious to tell him of her despair at his absence and to show him her weaving. Instead of accusing her as he had planned, he soon finds himself on the defensive against her jealousy of the goddesses he had loved. He explains, however, that it was always the dear image of Penelope that he had felt himself embracing. How succinctly Giono sums up their amorous reconciliation: "Odysseus withstood valiantly the onset of happiness."

The next morning they discover that Kalidassa, certain that her beloved had been killed by Odysseus and fearful of his revenge for her perfidy, has hanged herself from a tree. Lagobolon, the swine merchant, has spread word through the town concerning the vengeance of Odysseus: "He is stronger than they say. All at once he became very tall, very handsome, and such muscles! There is surely something god-like in him." Suddenly the dried-up spring, which had once furnished the town with water, begins to flow again; and the townspeople think this event is due to the beneficial, divine power of Odysseus. Recognizing now the power of his lies, he takes pleasure in fabricating them for the enraptured villagers: "And he left them intoxicated with images in a strange country where the clouds were wingèd bulls. One could hear under the mountains the roaring of divine forges, and, towards the horizon, an immense flute was set murmuring by the breath of Pan." The singing at olive gatherings was now replaced by bards engaged to recite the adventures of Odysseus, and the hands worked twice as fast: "Thus Odysseus was like an almond tree in blossom midst the plowed land which covers the black earth with light, fragrant petals."

In the meantime, Telemachus returns in sorry plight from his trip to Egypt. After narrowly escaping death at the hands of the natives—who even in those days seemed allergic to Europeans— he had been kidnapped by pirates who had starved him and had forced him to act as a decoy in his naked and emaciated condition to attract charitable rescuers whose ships could then be plundered. Poor Telemachus can talk of nothing but his sufferings, much to the boredom and incredulity of all who hear him. A final ironic touch is given when Kallimaques, a visiting philosopher who is now in the hog business and who is wearied by the recital of Telemachus' woes, ejaculates: "These young fellows have a fine imagination. Master Odysseus, give us a change from these artful inventions; I need to hear something which smacks of reality. Won't you be so courteous as to relate one of your adventures?"

VI *Evaluation*

It is obvious from the résumé that Giono, despite his admiration for Homer, had tongue in cheek while inventing this modern version of the legend. The underlying theme, of course, is the power of words and the virtue of lies; for Odysseus has invented his own legend and, as a result, is able to triumph over enemies stronger than he. Most critics find in this approach of Giono only the rollicking, fun-loving zest of youthful creativity; but Pugnet sees rather the beginning of Giono's tendency to criticize our civilization and its mores: "His [Odysseus'] lie conveys the need of old age to create illusory values to subdue the strength of youth." [3] And Pugnet also points to the recurrence of this idea in a later volume *Le Poids du ciel* in regard to education and propaganda. Another favorite theme of Giono in *Naissance de l'Odyssée*, one underscored by Pugnet, is to have the world of nature "in its totality or concentrated in a single element intervene in the play of characters to exercise a benevolent or malevolent action. It has a romantic, even a moral function. To those whose cause is just or who are close to it in their purity, it gives its aid or friendship." As an illustration, he mentions the crumbling of the cliff which kills Antinoüs and miraculously saves Odysseus. We might add to this the sudden flowing of the spring which makes the villagers feel they owe their good fortune to the return of Odysseus.

Another interesting feature of the *Naissance de l'Odyssée* is its early adumbration of certain qualities of the author which were to lie dormant for many years only to reappear in his recent so-called "second manner" of the *Chroniques*. As Chonez has so keenly observed, "This smiling apology for lying, this joy of story telling for the story itself, this humor full of wisdom, will not reappear for a long time under Giono's pen. Its current is, so to speak, interrupted by the ardent love of the earth, of the stars, of the charm of the seasons, of the rams, of the mountains, and also of the men who love all that. But it remains underneath; we shall see it resurgent twenty years later with the vagabonds, the horsemen, the charmers and the liars of the *Chroniques*." And, finally, we may prize *La Naissance* for its revelation of some aspects of Giono's own personality; for, as Lucien Jacques remarked with a mischievous twinkle in his eye, the character of Odysseus is really a somewhat unflattering portrait of Giono himself.

However, the style is even more important than the ideas to our enjoyment of this youthful work; it is exuberant in its zest for life, and it is brimming over with beauteous images and metaphors. As Michelfelder has pointed out, this novel is written like a poem: "The meaning is evident, but what pleasure to read it in order to let oneself be intoxicated by this style which is that of a musician rather than that of a writer, this style like the wine of Dionysus, warm and powerful." [4] In the chronology of his life which Giono furnished Claudine Chonez for her book, we find the entry: "1928 Grasset refuse *Naissance de l'Odyssée* (et il fait bien)." If this is proof that publishers are not infallible, it must be added that Grasset hastened to redeem his error of judgment by publishing *Naissance* in 1930 after the dazzling success of Giono's *Colline*.

CHAPTER 4

Trilogy of Pan

I Colline

AS André Rousseaux wrote in his *Littérature du XXième siècle,*
"The legendary voice which, according to Plutarch, cried
upon the waters 'Great Pan is Dead' spread one of the most nota-
ble pieces of misinformation which have resounded in the world's
history. Great Pan is still alive. The books of M. Giono are the
proof. The breath of the divine animal animates with its very
rhythm this rustic, poetic and pagan literature." [1]

Steeped in the translations of Homer and the Greek tragic poets
from his earliest youth and undaunted by the failure of his first
novel *Naissance de l'Odyssée* to find a publisher, Jean Giono, still
an humble bank clerk in his native town of Manosque, conceived
the plan for the three rustic novels constituting his *Trilogy of Pan.*
When the first of these, *Colline,* appeared in 1928 in an obscure
literary magazine in Paris, André Gide enthusiastically announced
to the world that a Virgil in prose had been born in Provence.
Even before its appearance in book form the following year, *Colline* was already famous. The biographical statement on the fly
leaf is a model of succinctness, written with tongue in cheek:
"Jean Giono, able to read and write, not able to swim."

These lines from Giono's preface to *Colline*—"When I had
planned to say what I knew about Pan, it seemed to me that sorrow should have the first, the great place; it seemed to me that
Pan consisted above all of this terror and this cruelty"—help to set
the atmosphere for this strange tale in which the superstitions of
the lonely peasants are mingled with the sense of fatality, of revenge which the earth takes upon man for his thoughtless and
placid complacency. To quote the preface again: "All the errors of
man come from his imagining that he treads an inert thing when
his steps are imprinted into flesh full of great will." Most critics
have pointed out that Pan, the *enfant terrible* who does not wish
to be forgotten, is symbolized in this story by the spring on whose

flowing the lives of this tiny mountain hamlet depend. We shall see, however, from a résumé of the action that the element of fire plays a role as destructive and even more terrifying than that of water.

In addition to the harmless idiot Gagou, four families are living a peaceful existence in the isolated hamlet of Les Bastides. The dour octogenarian Janet begins to talk mysteriously after a paralytic seizure as if out of his head concerning the strange life of trees, plants, animals, and even stones. He warns the villagers of approaching danger because they have not realized the cruelty that they have inflicted on nature. Giono succeeds masterfully in making the readers share the growing apprehension of the peasants as each new incident brings with it a sense of uneasy foreboding. When Gondron, in his olive grove, kills a lizard with his spade, he suddenly recalls the imprecations of old Janet, who claimed that everything was alive: "So he can no longer raise his finger without making torrents of sorrow run." Suddenly the village notices a strange silence; the communal spring has ceased to flow. Several days' search for water is without avail until one night the villagers follow Gagou stealthily to a ghost town far up the mountain which still has its flowing fountain. From it, they bring back jars of water to the hamlet.

Soon, however, they are threatened by a greater catastrophe, a forest fire sweeping over the mountain. As their petty bickering and jealousies melt away before the menace to their village, the men fight night and day with almost superhuman energy to keep away the flames; but they are saved only by a last-minute change in the wind. Suspected by the villagers as the cause of this mysterious animosity of the forces of nature, old Janet dies just as they reluctantly decide to kill him; and, at the moment of his death, they hear outside a familiar sound: the spring has once more begun to flow. Yet never again will they be able to take nature for granted, and their joy in their newfound security is darkened by the discovery of the idiot's body burned to a crisp by the conflagration.

According to Jacques Pugnet in his book on Giono, the author in writing *Colline* did not start from the idea of a vindictive god, but rather thought first of the spring, the fragile thread of water on which the lives of families depended: "The image of the fragility and the power of the nourishing water, encountered in his thought the notion of the sovereign but versatile god. The spring became incarnate in the god; it personified it rather than symbolized it. The true poet goes from the element to the myth which it suggests; he does not start from a culture but rediscovers it."

Although the language of Giono in *Colline*, as indeed in all three novels of the trilogy, is simple and direct—far removed from the effervescent exuberance of his later manner—nevertheless the atmosphere is one of haunting beauty in which the mountain of Lure plays a large part. The great charm of style in *Colline* is Giono's capacity for choosing metaphors which are striking, breathtaking in their novelty without being precious or extravagant, and which almost always associate the characteristics of animals or even human beings with physical objects and elements. Thus in speaking of the rain "basted with arrows from the sun, beaten by the rough hand of the wind," he states that "its warm feet have crushed the oats." The water of the spring is likewise an animate force: "if you listen closely, you can hear its furtive step; it glides gently from the meadow to the path on the tip of its little white feet." Even abstractions take on the quality of concrete picturesque imagery: "the earliest risers are the pigeons; the dawn juggles with them with its soft hands." To Giono's perceptive eye nature is ever changing, ever new. Thus one morning when "a thick crown of violets presses down on the pure brow of the sky, the sun rises like a pomegranate through this mist." On another occasion, "the sun with a single leap leaves the ground of the horizon and enters the sky like a wrestler balancing on its arms of fire." The sky of Giono's Provence is likewise limitless in its poetic diversity. At times it reminds him of "a great blue whetstone which sharpens the scythes of grasshoppers." Again, during a storm, the sky becomes "the arena of noise; chariots' mares with steelshod hoofs appear then with rumbling gallop and angry neighing."

Giono is at his best in portraying nature in her more violent moods, when in storm or in forest fire she seems to come alive like some primeval monster to threaten presumptuous human beings who have been lulled into careless indifference. "The storm like a bull whipped with grasses tore itself away from the mud of the plains; it swelled its muscular back; then it jumped over the hills and began its course through the sky." The description of the forest fire, unsurpassed perhaps by anything else Giono has written for dramatic intensity, is too long for quotation here, but mention must at least be made of the fascination of this brilliant spectacle for Gagou, of whom it makes an involuntary suicide: "He approaches, holds out his hands; and, in spite of the fiery vice which crushes his feet, he advances into the land of the thousand candelabra of gold." From these quotations it is not too difficult to understand Gide's conviction that a new literary star had appeared in the firmament.

II Un de Baumugnes (1929)

The second novel of the trilogy, *Un de Baumugnes*, is, as Brodin has said, "a love story told by a peasant in a rustic and vigorous style which again recalls the Homeric poems." [2] If *Colline* shows us the cruelty and terror of Pan, *Un de Baumugnes* on the other hand is bathed in sunlight and warmth, an idyl of human friendship and selfless devotion. As Michelfelder reminds us: "Pan is not only a terrifying god, he is also the inventor of a flute, the syrinx." In this story, however, the flute is represented by the harmonica.

Amédée, the peasant who tells the story, meets young Albin, whose heart has been broken several years before when a dapper, smooth-spoken city rival had seduced the girl he loved and persuaded her to elope with him for a life of debauchery. Deeply moved by Albin's misery, Amédée sends him to the farm of a friend and promises to bring him news of the young woman. Arriving at the desolate and ill-kept farm of La Douloire where Angèle had lived, Amédée offers his services to the owner, a stern old man with one arm in a sling, whose wife finally persuades him to accept the offer. With his courage and industry Amédée soon restores the farm economy; but,·as he is about to admit his mission to be fruitless, he receives confirmation of his suspicions that Angèle is sequestered somewhere on the premises. Obtaining a few days' leave, he brings back Albin, whom he hides in the neighborhood.

Albin is a native of the little town of Baumugnes high up in the mountains where his Huguenot ancestors had taken refuge and learned to play harmonicas after their tongues had been cut out so that they could no longer speak and carry on their heresy. Albin himself has inherited this musical faculty; and, seated on the trunk of a gnarled tree in front of the silo, he plays melodies evocative of the beauty of stream and forest which strangely move all the occupants of the farmhouse. Angèle recognizes the presence of the young man she had known before her seduction; and, by scratching on the wall of her prison, she makes Albin understand her incarceration. With the aid of Amédée, she and her ten-month-old baby are released by Albin, and they flee in the night. Realizing, however, that Clarius, her father, will probably drown himself from shame and despair, they return by daylight in spite of the danger that they will be shot. When a reconciliation has been effected, the lovers set forth once more with the blessings of the old parents, who now feel that the shame from which they suffered has been removed by their daughter's opportunity for a life of honorable love.

It is impossible in a bald recital of the story to give an idea of its deeply moving pathos and human compassion. As Professor Peyre has written, "The story is simple but told with consummate art, with none of the complex layers of motives and desires dear to the novels of the nineteen-thirties. It is credible throughout, flowing with life. Unashamedly it portrayed in postwar literature a man who was sincerely and naïvely in love and a woman worthy of being loved."

Since the recital is given by a peasant, Giono's style here is of necessity even simpler than in *Colline;* at times it is full of slang and grammatical improprieties. Yet Amédée, untutored farm laborer though he may be, is a man sensitive to natural beauty: "In the depth of my being, I belong to the land, heavy with wheat, with cypress trees against the little farmhouses, with clumps of live oaks, with grass made russet by the sun and with empty brooks in which flow instead of water the noise of carts, the perfume of wild thyme and the laughter of goat-herders." Through the perception of this humble peasant Giono makes us feel the thrill of rustic sensations in everyday life, as for instance in the description of the installation of Albin in his hiding place: "We hang up the knapsacks, arrange the pallet, clean out the fireplace and start a big pine branch blazing in the way of welcome. The odor of resin and the grease of sausage spitting on the coals made the morning festive, and then the rising sun came over the door-step like a golden pigeon. Birds were darting from every bush. How beautiful life was." In no other work perhaps has Giono excelled this transfiguration of humble reality into the essence of poetry, and we are reminded of the verse of Rupert Brooke and of passages in Saint-Exupéry's *Wind, Sand and Stars* and *Flight to Arras.*

In *Colline,* nature is the true protagonist; and the human characters, except for the picturesque silhouettes of the mystic octogenarian Janet and the idiot Gagou, are not too clearly differentiated. In *Un de Baumugnes,* however, in spite of the realistic background of rustic life, the individuals have distinct personalities which stamp themselves on our memory. First, of course, is the narrator Amédée, the earliest of that long line of *"guerisseurs"* or healers inspired by the character of Giono's own father, whom we find in many of his later books: "Since the evening before, that furious suffering had given me my usual malady, my malady for being of service." Though Albin in gratitude for Amédée's aid in rescuing Angèle calls him "the grandfather of happiness," Amédée is not an idealized abstraction but a creature of flesh and blood who is not averse on occasion to sharing the couch of a farmer's wife.

Louis, the vile seducer, is but lightly sketched and seems to represent the vice and corruption of an urban civilization as opposed to the robust sanity and purity of the country represented by Albin. The latter indeed, "tall, with eyes of clear water and laughter like the snow," is one of Giono's most sympathetic characterizations. If Albin is pure in heart, it is because he incarnates the nobility of his native village high up in the mountains: "As for me, I have all Baumugnes inside me, and it is heavy, because it is made of thick earth which touches the sky, and trees which shoot up straight, but it is good, it is beautiful, it is broad and clean, it is made of spotless sky, of good thick hay and of air sharpened like a saber." Albin too is a *"guérisseur"* for he plays his ineffable melodies not for his delight alone but "for healing man and woman and the daughters of the earth." We may think Albin almost too noble in his willingness to overlook Angèle's past of prostitution and to adopt her fatherless child, yet we find him capable of fierce anger against her seducer: "What I reproach Baumugnes for, my village which made me, is that it did not teach me to kill. That would have taken a minute, one little minute."

As Michelfelder has written, *Un de Baumugnes* represents the second aspect of Pan, "the beautiful singer in the suite of Dionysus, who makes the nymphs dance and Silenus laugh—after the terrifying cry of the earth, here is its song of joy and purity; the terror of Pan and the gentleness of Pan. *Regain* will synthesize them both in a strongly flavored symphony."

III Regain

The third volume of Giono's *Trilogy of Pan, Regain* (1930, entitled *Harvest* in its English translation) is perhaps the best known to Anglo-Saxons through its very successful movie version. Though not without its episodes of bitter realism and sorrow, it is in the main an idealistic portrayal of the awakening of nature, both of the earth and of man himself. As Michelfelder says, "this is the book of Pan, the one in which the god is immediately present as if fused in all things. Pan borrows, in order to orchestrate the novel, his natural voice, the wind: the wind which shouts its fury on the plateau or whispers its song at evening in the reeds." It is interesting to learn that the first title of this book was *Winds of Spring*, under which name excerpts actually appeared in magazine form.

In *Regain*, the tiny village of Aubignane, "glued against the edge of the plateau like a little wasp's nest," has seen its discouraged inhabitants leave it one by one until only three persons are left. One of them, le Panturle, "is an enormous man. One would say a piece of wood walking. In the midst of summer when he makes a cover for his neck with fig leaves, when with his hands full of grass he stands up straight, his arms stretched out, to look at the earth, he is a tree. His shirt hangs in shreds like a bark. He has big, thick shapeless lips like a red pimiento." He makes his living by hunting and dwells alone since the death of his aged mother. Gaubert is a tiny mustached old man who lives in his ruined smithy, once renowned for its manufacture of plowshares in the days when the land was still under cultivation. Mamèche is a tragically somber old woman who had come here long before from Italy with her husband, who had been killed when a well he was digging for the villagers collapsed and inundated him. When the solitude of the village has been deepened by the departure of the aged blacksmith to seek the care of his children, old Mamèche also sets out to bring back a woman for Panturle in order that the village may survive.

Plodding their painful way across the boundless bareness of the plateau, Gédémus, the old knife-sharpener, and Arsule, the young woman who pulls his cart, are terrified by the wind which almost tears the clothes from their bodies and are mystified by a strange apparition (which we later find to be Mamèche) hopping in front of them and then suddenly disappearing. In their efforts to escape this disturbing phenomenon, they are driven off their normal route and close to Aubignane where they are seen by Panturle, who decides to intercept them by taking a short cut to the falls. Perched high in a tree to await their arrival, he is catapulted into the stream by a broken branch and is washed over the rapids. Regaining consciousness some hours later, he learns that the couple had arrived just in time to pull him from the water. The knife-sharpener has gone to sleep but Arsule, full of tenderness for the man she has saved, yields to his embrace and consents to go back with him to Aubignane.

Soon the lonely house begins to take on order and domesticity under a woman's helpful hands. Le Panturle descends to the valley to borrow wheat for seeding, a horse, and a plough. In the following autumn Panturle brings to the fair in Banon six sacks of the most beautiful grain ever seen and for which he receives a fabulous price since the harvest elsewhere that year had been scarce and of pitiful quality. Soon a family with children come to reside in Aubignane, drawn by their desire to settle on the land and to emulate Panturle's success. Arsule is deeply affected by the laughter of the three children, and the next spring Panturle learns with joy that his home also will be enlivened by the same sounds.

Professor Peyre feels that the ending of *Regain* partakes too much of a fairy tale, with too obvious a moral lesson which detracts from the artistic quality, though he admits this was rendered more palatable in the moving picture version. A mere résumé of the action may indeed give this impression, but the earthy realism of the setting and the sincerity of the characters make the tale credible and highly moving. There are few passages in literature more accurate in their detail than the multi-colored description of the country fair at Banon, which brings to mind Flaubert's famous depiction of the *comices agricoles* in *Madame Bovary*. As Pugnet has pointed out, even though Giono is fond of introducing fantastic adventures into his novels, his personages never act without profound reasons, such as a necessity or the demands of a passion: "One of the essential themes is the struggle for life, the search for normal conditions of existence. . . . *Regain* is the toil for bread and the seeking for a wife."

If Giono has been attracted by the legendary side of myths, Pugnet reminds us that legends, superstitions, and traditional practices are abundant in peasant novels: "Giono recalls them perhaps only to represent the profound immobility of peasant society and thereby he raises the latter out of all temporality. Evoked also in their perennial quality, myths symbolize in a sense the eternity of nature." It is obvious that Giono had in mind as he wrote *Regain* the figure of Demeter, whom Michelfelder terms "the goddess of the fruitful earth, who breathes amply through her vast breast of plateaux with 'the everlasting wind' and causes the beautiful shiny wheat to germinate."

IV *The Trilogy*

For all of their diversity of plot and atmosphere, the three novels which make up Giono's *Trilogy of Pan* have an essential unity of inspiration, one which is characteristic of all of the works belonging to his so-called "first manner" lasting down to the outbreak of World War II. To quote his critic and biographer Claudine Chonez: "If there is in the work of Giono a 'leitmotif' from the first works to those of today, it is indeed that of the harsh and bare earth. But whereas a Mauriac would associate it with the hardness of life, with sadness and solitude, Giono sees in it the symbol of the fecund struggle, as well as of liberty and immediate communion; naked man against naked earth." Rousseaux likewise stresses this fundamental unity of Giono when he states that all of his early work is only a "Presentation of Pan: of Pan in his first nudity before his breath was modified by any reed." [3] It is something of a paradox that out of our blasé and sophisticated civilization with its refinement of gadgets and superfluities there should have arisen this solitary figure of a man still in communion with the simple and elemental forces of nature. Perhaps that very strangeness and anomaly account for Giono's hold on our imagination today.

CHAPTER 5

Friendship with André Gide

I   *A Visit to Manosque*

IN 1930 *Colline*, translated into English by Jacques Leclerq under the title *Hill of Destiny*, won the Prix Brentano of a thousand dollars. As explained by the translator in his introduction, this was the first American foundation to crown a French work and to insure its publication in America. The fact that the jury included no Frenchmen gave evidence, as he remarked, that the choice was not due to the maneuvers of cliques which often control French prize awards. The following year *Un de Baumugnes*, translated into English as *Lovers Are Never Losers*, received the Northcliff award in Great Britain.

It will be recalled that the meteoric success of *Colline* was due in large measure to the rhapsodic eulogies of André Gide, who had read it first in the literary revue *Commerce*. It is interesting to note that on at least one other occasion Gide's enthusiastic intervention had helped to launch the successful career of a young writer—his Preface for *Night Flight* by Antoine de Saint-Exupéry. When Gide died in 1952 and the memorial volume *Hommage à André Gide* was under consideration, Giono was one of the authors selected to write a chapter on his memories of Gide, an essay which furnishes many intimate revelations concerning the warm personal friendship which developed between these men.

The first time Giono had met Gide was on the occasion of the former's first visit to Paris in 1928 to sign the publicity for *Colline* at his publishers. The writer André Chamson had arranged a dinner for Giono, to which Léon-Paul Fargue, Adrienne Monnier, Jean Guéhenno, and the Russian Ilya Ehrenburg were invited, as well as Gide. On this occasion the inexperienced Giono quite naturally did everything that he should not have done. In particular, during the course of a long conversation with Gide who had asked him about his future plans, he had related to him in great detail the plot of his next story, *Un de Baumugnes*. "The books that one narrates well are generally failures," was Gide's rather discouraging comment.

In 1927 Giono had moved from the old dwelling on the Grand' Rue to the fourth floor of a building at number 1, Boulevard de la Plaine, of which the ground floor was occupied by offices. Here one day in 1929 he heard his mother calling him to state that "a very nice tall man was waiting for him in the dining room, saying his name was Gide." Unfortunately, Giono was able to remain with Gide only five minutes since his work at the bank demanded his presence. Gide, however, seemed to understand the circumstances, asked Giono to recommend a hotel, and promised to remain several days if Giono could arrange a few walks with him through the countryside. Very much touched by his visit, Giono spent his noon hour with Gide at the hotel, the latter postponing his siesta; and Giono found him again at six in the little narrow corridor of the apartment which was the only place Giono had been able to reserve for his library. While waiting, Gide had examined Giono's collection; though he found none of his own writings there, he congratulated Giono on the choice of books he had acquired in the course of twenty years. Noticing a few English books, including a volume of Whitman, he asked Giono if he could read English and, on receiving an affirmative answer, advised him to read Browning. A few days after his departure Giono received from him a pocket edition of the poems and dramas of Robert Browning, which became a frequent companion on his travels.

During the five or six days that Gide remained in Manosque they took many walks together on the hillside, talking not of literature but of trees and flowers. On this subject they had many controversies, for Gide showed himself to be an admirable botanist and Giono, who prided himself on his botanical knowledge, found himself frequently in error, except in regard to trees.

On March 29 of the same year Giono received a letter from Gide, thanking him for his declarations of friendship and congratulating him for not having expressed it earlier; for his having done so might have embarrassed Gide in his judgment of *Colline* and *Un de Baumugnes:* "I had no need of it in order to like you, and at that time I doubted that a reciprocal feeling was possible; but I am happy that you are grateful to me for understanding and praising you." Gide confessed that he had not been particularly fond of *Naissance de l'Odyssée* and that he had found, on the other hand, concentrated in the *Cahier de l'Artisan*—evidently the one containing *Accompagnés de la flûte*—the poetic qualities which were too scattered and diffused in the former. Gide concluded his letter by hoping that Giono, despite his shyness, would accept an invitation to attend a gathering that summer at Pontigny of thirty writers from different countries, including Roger Martin du Gard. There is no indication, however, that Giono accepted this invitation.

II *Reunion at Lalley*

Giono had the habit of spending his summer vacations in the mountains, and the next visit from Gide seems to have taken place in July, 1936, at Lalley, a little village some four kilometers distant from the railroad station of Saint-Maurice-en-Trièves. Gide, who had preferred to make these four kilometers on foot through the woods, arrived at noon with his little daughter Catherine, their arms full of flowers picked from the fields along the way. After a lunch of cold chicken, Gide took his siesta while Catherine, who greatly resembled her father, played with the ten-year-old Aline. Towards evening the two men walked with the children to a meadow high up beyond the gorges. All during the walk Giono had been wondering what it was that Gide was carrying in the pocket of his coat. When they sat down in the meadow in the sunlight, Gide pulled from his pocket the proofs of the next number of the *Nouvelle Revue Française* and read to Giono some recent pages of his *Journal*. Giono, filled with enthusiasm, found in them the answer to his most secret interrogations concerning Communism. He was impressed also with Gide's extraordinary preoccupation with God.

After refreshing his memory by reading his journal for the period 1935–36, Giono recalls, in his article for the memorial volume *Hommage à André Gide*, the large house they occupied at Lalley, cold, somber and uncomfortable, covered with a broad roof which descended almost to the ground. It was heated by a roaring wood-stove which the family nourished with ash shavings and sawdust. When Giono went twice a week to obtain kindling from the sawmill, Gide walked beside the wheelbarrow. He seemed to take great pleasure in sitting in the shade on the bench near the spring, in watching the horses, in playing *boules* with

Giono and his friend Gaston Peloux, and in working in his room next to that of Giono; for Gide was finishing at this time *Les Nouvelles Nourritures*. Giono was impressed, as were all the inhabitants of Lalley, with the great human value of Gide. Giono became very fond of Gide, though he insists that Gide had no influence on his own solitary career, since he had read little by him other than his *Journal*. Apparently his frank admission of this fact did not disturb Gide's attitude in the least. Were it not for Giono's categorical denial, the literary critic would be tempted to seek a repercussion of Gide's *Nourritures Terrestres* on Giono's own period of exaltation of natural instincts, but apparently this is only a case of remarkable affinity, explaining in large measure Giono's attraction for Gide.

An amusing anecdote concerning Gide's visit at Lalley is related in *Voyage en Italie*. Gide was very fond of chess, and the two friends often played in the back room of a little mountain bistro. One of Giono's rustic friends named Bergues had the habit of seating himself near the players to watch the progress of the match. Never saying a word, he would deposit three or four frogs on the table near the chess board. Because of the coolness of the table they remained quite motionless. Then from time to time Bergues would swallow one of the frogs alive, wash it down with a large glass of wine, and depart in silence after completing his strange repast. Apparently this byplay irritated Gide extremely, and as a result Giono was able to enjoy several checkmates.

One afternoon when Giono returned from taking his friend Denoel to the station he found Gide seated on the green bench before the door, reading a copy of Giono's novel *Que ma joie demeure*. Gide said: "I have no longer any reservation in regard to the style," and he praised the musical composition of the work with its retards and largos. Then he offered to read a few pages of what he expected to be his last book, *Les Nouvelles Nourritures*, which impressed Giono greatly with its beauty, its lofty lyricism, its intelligent humanity. That evening they went with Catherine and Aline to the rustic bistro where Gide read aloud from the letters of Lewis Carroll. When it came time for Gide to leave for Geneva, the two friends embraced with great emotion.

III Final Meetings

The loyal affection which Gide felt for Giono was proved later on at least two occasions. To anticipate in our narrative, Gide rallied to Giono's side at the time of his imprisonment at the beginning of World War II and was in part responsible for Giono's liberation. Again after the war was over he urged leniency for Giono, Montherlant, Céline, and other authors accused of defeatism; he reminded the Resistance writers that his own attitude as expressed in his *Journal* of that period had been exactly the same as that of Giono.[1]

The last time Giono saw his friend was in 1949, but ten years of correspondence had followed their meeting in December, 1939, after Giono's liberation from prison. To Lucien Jacques, whom he had encountered during a sojourn at Saint-Paul de Vence, Gide had expressed a desire to see Giono once more. On this occasion Gide showed himself so affectionate that for the first time Giono had the courage to express himself without restraint or shyness. Before going to drink together their glasses of *pastis*, Gide gave to each of them, Giono and Lucien Jacques, copies of what he called "his final writings."

CHAPTER 6

Two Semi-Autobiographical Novels

I Le Grand Troupeau

AS stated earlier, Giono, like many of his generation, was never able to erase from his consciousness the horror of his four years in the trenches, and his realization of the utter futility and stupidity of modern war. From his demobilization in 1919, as he tells us many years later in *Refus de l'obéissance,* he carried on his campaign against war with everyone—his own family, his friends, and his enemies—even at the risk of losing his humble position as a bank clerk and of being labeled a Communist. In 1930, encouraged by the success of his *Trilogy of Pan,* he had taken the bold step of resigning his position of almost twenty years and of purchasing a home, Le Paraïs, on the slope of Le Mont d'Or where he still dwells today. The first novel in which he expresses his bitter excoriation of war is *Le Grand Troupeau* (1931), a work intensely subjective in nature since it reflects in large measure his own experience under the guise of its chief protagonist, Olivier.

The most epic scene in the book, one of the most powerful and moving passages Giono has ever written, is the opening chapter which shows us the apparently endless procession of sheep and lambs coming down from the high plateaux and streaming painfully through the little Provençal town. Since all the young shepherds have been summoned to war, the two old *baïles* who remain are compelled to drive their flocks down from the cool, green pastures in the mountains, where they would have passed the summer, to the hot, dry corrals in the valley. Flecked with dirt and sweat under the blistering sun, their hides cracked and bleeding, the vast herd excites the deepest compassion as it plods valiantly forward. Especially poignant is the distress of the venerable ram as he tries to rest his heavy head on the backs of two sheep which precede him before he dies along the wayside. One of the old shepherds, overcome with pity and remorse for his own ram, implores one of the peasants to keep it for him and nurse it back to health. Robert Brasillach has called this farewell of the shepherd to his ram as beautiful as that of Cyclops to his beast in Canto Nine of the *Odyssey*.[1] Compelling in its own right for its epic evocation, this picture of the demoralization of the herd is of course symbolic of the book's tragic theme, for we think at once of that other herd of helpless men dragged off to the exhaustion and suffering of war.

It would be too much, perhaps, to expect the rest of the book to continue on the same lofty tone; and most critics have found the remaining scenes, which alternate between war at the front and life among those left behind, too episodic and disconnected for a well-constructed novel. The propaganda purpose of the author is perhaps a little too evident, and Mondadon[2] is justified when he writes, after praising Giono's gift for colorful images: "but his visual temperament and his passionate enthusiasm carry him away sometimes to brutal descriptions and his bold brush does not recoil before any detail, however ignoble." Horrible indeed are some of the battlefield scenes, with rats and vultures eating human flesh. Yet it is only fair to add that there are also several episodes of quiet pathos, such as the fraternal watch kept by Joseph for a day and a night over his dying comrade while awaiting the ambulance which did not come; or the gentleness of the French officer in receiving the captured German prisoner who expected execution; or, finally, the rapport which springs up between Olivier and another peasant soldier through their mutual concern for the trees whose bark the horses were nibbling.

If the war scenes seem inferior in artistry to those of Duhamel in *Vie des martyrs* and in *Civilisation,* the passages dealing with pastoral life represent Giono at his best. Unforgettable in its simple pathos is the wake or vigil held for the widow's husband, dead on some distant battlefield. The tragic consequences of war are most visible among those who stayed home: the wives and fiancées on daily watch for the mayor's messenger announcing fatalities; the schoolteacher who dismissed her little flock the day she was apprised of her brother's death; the draft board forced to accept the epileptic lad because he possessed the necessary weight and height. Pitiful indeed were those who returned disabled by loss of limb, among them Casimir who awaited the day when he could replace his crutch with an iron leg jointed at the knee: "Julia looks at this pale, soft man. Casimir has lost the ruddiness of men of the sun, he has the fat, white hands of those who have been fed soup, with only the trouble to open their mouths, and who grow stout on their chair, like sacks. A handsome ploughman he had been before, thin and wiry like an old bean." Giono's pity is stirred likewise by the changed countryside, abandoned to the frail care of women, old men, and children: "The fields with that sparse wheat, like a young man's beard; that yellow, anemic wheat, here in tufts, there with wide-open spaces; that wheat sown by a woman's hand; that wheat of a child. How strong the weeds, since all knowledge and skill had been lost. Since those who were expert and had healthy arms had been sent away in a big herd to their death."

Louis de Mondadon has called this novel a triptych: the caravan of the great herd forms the central piece; and, on the two sides, are scenes of war and of the countryside. It would be more accurate, perhaps, to think of the descent of the sheep as the prologue, followed by the war itself with its contrasting scenes of carnage and rural life, and concluded by an epilogue in which we see the return of the old shepherd to reclaim his ram, once more vigorous and healthy. This visit of the shepherd coincides with the birth of a son to Madeleine and her regained soldier, Olivier. When the old shepherd causes his ram to breathe upon the newborn babe so that he too will be "one who leads, one who goes forward, not one who follows" and wishes him all true blessings, this novel, which began with an ominous symbol and contained so many scenes of sorrow and bloodshed, ends with a lyric paean of hope for the future: "If God may listen to me, it will be thy lot to love slowly, slowly in all thy loves, like one who holds the shafts of the plow and digs a little more deeply each day. Thou wilt never weep the watery tear through thy eyes, but, like the vine, through the cleft opened at random. Thou wilt often carry the burden of others, and be by the roadside like a fountain. And thou wilt love the stars."

II   Jean le bleu (Blue Boy, 1932)

Blue Boy, even more directly a reflection of his own experience than *Le Grand Troupeau*, relates the spiritual development of the author from earliest childhood to his departure for the first world war. Henry Miller in *The Books in My Life* has indeed termed it "The Story Teller's Story" because it gives us "the physiology, the chemistry, the physics, the biology of that curious animal, the writer . . . connects us with the source of all creative activity." [3]

Clearly visible in *Blue Boy* is the fact that Giono's sensuousness, the development of which he ascribes to his father's delicate surveillance, is a cardinal feature of his art. "I know that I am a sensualist," confesses Jean le bleu. "If one has the humility to call upon one's instinct, upon the elemental, there is in sensuousness a kind of cosmic joy." A result of this extreme sensuousness is that, as Peyre has put it, "the book overflows with vitality; the very images are heavy, like pendant clusters of grapes." The reader of *Blue Boy* may be startled by this unconventional imagery, sometimes a little far-fetched and labored, more often of the highest poetic quality as in this sentence: "In the summer, towards noon, a drop of sunlight slipped into the court like a wasp and then flew off." Like Zola, with whom he is racially akin but whom he does not particularly admire, Giono may shock one at times with his naturalistic detail and frankness; but this occasional crudeness only enhances by contrast the poetic richness of his sensuous imagery and the haunting, plaintive undertone of his mystic wonder at life.

Closely related to this quality in *Blue Boy* is the parallel theme of music. In fact, this very sensuousness, according to Giono, prevented him from learning music, "putting a higher price on the intoxication of listening than on the joy of being skilled." It is pleasant to learn from Miss Clarke[4] that those two quaint and lovable eccentrics, Décidément and Madame la Reine, whose rendition of Bach and Mozart on flute and violin lend such enchantment to the book, really existed; they are a fanciful and poetic idealization of Giono's own father. The names are taken, she informs us, from the phrase in Dumas' melodrama: "Décidément, Madame la Reine, il fera noir ce soir à la tour de Nesle." This passion for music and particularly for Mozart was to become one of the leitmotifs of Giono's life and is responsible for the unusual sense of harmony and counterpoint which pervades his books, causing critics to liken several of them to symphonies. As Henry Miller has written: "In Giono the instrument and the music are one. That is his special gift. If he did not become a musician because as he says, he thought it more important to be a good listener, he has become a writer who has raised listening to such an

art that we follow his melodies as if we had written them ourselves."

In addition to its autobiographical reflections, *Jean le bleu* also
relates stories of the simple inhabitants of Giono's little town and
countryside—shepherds, bakers, musicians, and all the humble
tradesmen of the area. Apparently the simplest and most natural
of Giono's books, it nevertheless gives an impression of extraordinary human profundity. Lacking the well-balanced unity of a
carefully composed novel, "it meanders," writes Henri Peyre,
"among the profuse reminiscences of the author's childhood,
treasures the sounds and smells through which young Jean awoke
to the exterior world, and conjures up, in an order as capriciously
alien to time sequences as that of Proust's saga, visions of nature,
farmers and animals, all reeling in a dizzy feast of the senses,
amid the pagan setting of upper Provence." Some of these episodes are filled with pitiful tragedy, as in the case of the love-
starved Mexican woman or of Francesc Odripano's mother, who
is forced to drink, herself, the poisoned lemonade she had prepared for her cruel in-laws. Others are boldly comic, such as the
famous adventure of the *Baker's Wife*, better known to most Anglo-Saxons in Pagnol's movie version.

What gives a certain unity, however, to the rambling incidents
and recurrent themes of *Jean le bleu* is the admirable figure of old
Jean-Antoine, now appearing as the gentle and philosophic shoemaker, now as the musicians mentioned above, or as the imaginative Italian dreamer, Francesc Odripano. Shining through the
stark realism of the tortured lives of the rustic inhabitants is the
noble idealism of Giono's father, who cobbled shoes in his spare
time but whose real purpose in life was to heal the wounds, moral
as well as physical, he found around him. It would be easy to
agree with Miss Clarke, the translator, that *Jean le bleu* contains
the most beautiful homage that a son has ever paid his father
were it not for the fact that, in his later books, Giono was to equal
if not surpass this tribute.

CHAPTER 7

Three Rustic Dramas

I Le Bout de la route

TO some it may come as a surprise to learn that Giono, prolific and successful novelist, has also been tempted by the stage. That this is not, as was the case with writers such as Vigny and Balzac, a mere fleeting interest soon to be overshadowed by work in other genres is proved by the fact that Giono's preoccupation with the theater goes back to his short *Esquisse d'une mort d'Hélène* written in his twenty-fifth year; it continues down to the present with his recent ventures in radio drama and cinema. This penchant for the dramatic genre is all the more surprising because, in the opinion of all his critics (except that of Romée de Villeneuve who finds everything Giono writes equally felicitous), his gifts are primarily those of a descriptive artist and inventor of mysterious adventures. One would assume that Giono, when writing his dramas, would disregard stage conventions and content himself with closet drama; yet all of his plays have been performed with some success, one of them, at least, in several foreign countries.

Though the volume containing Giono's trilogy of rustic dramas was not published until 1943, the plays themselves were written in 1932–33 not long after his completion of the *Trilogy of Pan* with which they have many analogies. *Le Bout de la route,* first appearing in the second number of the *Cahiers du Contadour* in 1937, is almost devoid of action and is rather the painting of a mood in the manner of Jean-Jacques Bernard's Theater of Silence, as found, for instance, in *Martine* or *Invitation au voyage.*

In *Le Bout de la route,* it is late in the evening in a little hamlet backed up against a high mountain when Jean arrives weary from a long journey and seeks hospitality in a house at the end of the road. Here he finds the mountaineer Albert who descends every Tuesday to visit his fiancée Mina, the latter's mother Rosine, and the old grandmother half crazed with grief over the loss some years before of her daughter. Jean has no difficulty in establishing rapport with the aged crone, for he too has lost someone dear to him, the unfaithful spouse he had left behind in the embrace of another, but whose presence in his heart is so real that he perceives the existence of those around him only as shadows. Both Mina and Albert feel compassion for this lonely stranger, who is taken into the household and given work on the land. Soon we realize that Mina's pity for this handsome dreamer and idealist has changed to love; and Albert, conscious of the detachment of his fiancée, nobly assures Jean that he is still his friend. Rosine, moved by maternal tenderness for Jean's solitude, tries without avail to call him back into the world of the living; and, when Jean understands at last that Mina has lavished upon him a love he cannot share, he mournfully resumes his lonely pilgrimage to "the end of the road."

Both Michelfelder and Villeneuve have seen in the character of Jean a precursor of Bobi, the wandering poet, acrobat and idealist of *Que ma joie demeure*. Like Bobi, Jean is full of poetic imagery: "It must be a beautiful night all sprinkled with stars. The mountain in bloom opens like a fountain. The night glides over one gently like a great cloak." Yet Jean reminds us also of Albin, the hero of *Un de Baumugnes*, for he comes from the high mountains and he too is able to forgive the woman who has been unfaithful. There is something of Albin also in the gentle musician Albert— who plays an accordion rather than a harmonica. Villeneuve has pointed out the resemblance of Rosine to old Mamèche of *Regain*, whose desire for the perpetuation of the village had led her to bring together the hermit Panturle and the woman Arsule. Rosine, too, tries to awaken Jean to his responsibility as a living man and to draw him back from his shadow world of fidelity to a lost ideal.

As has been noted, the weakness of the play lies in its static quality. In the persons of the grandmother and of Rosine we have the conflict of two forces for the soul of Jean: sterility of the dead past refusing to accept reality, and the life force insisting upon eternal transformation and adaptation. Yet, in the heart of Jean, there is no real struggle; for he goes about his daily tasks like a man in a dream, more conscious of the woman he has lost than of the people of flesh and blood who surround him: "When I arrived here, Mina, you all took pity on me, because it was my first night in the tomb. If you only knew how cold it is, how full of fear.

How terrible it is to be alone." But, if there is no movement in this drama, it nevertheless is deeply moving in its simple pathos and resignation. Perhaps it is this quality which accounts for its run of more than five hundred performances in the Théâtre des Noctambules in Paris during the occupation.

II Lanceurs de graines

Lanceurs de graines is of all Giono's plays the most truly dramatic, the most harmoniously balanced in its combination of poetic atmosphere and symbol with sharply delineated characters. This play has contributed most to Giono's international reputation as a dramatist; after its first performance in Geneva in 1932, followed by those of the Théâtre de l'Atelier and the Théâtre Montmartre in Paris that same year, it was presented in London (both in French and English), in Brussels, Oslo, Frankfort, Prague, and Vienna.

As the curtain rises, we see Aubert preparing to leave the ancestral farm because, after his father's death, his mother had married Maître Antoine, a practical, hard-fisted realist determined to sacrifice the natural beauties of the estate in order to introduce efficient methods of cultivation. As the idealistic young Aubert, taught by his late father to thrill with the rustic charm of water rippling from the fountain and birds nestling in the foliage, reproaches his stepfather bitterly for his sacrilege in trying to master and violate the land, his mother cries: "One would say you are disputing for a woman." If Maître Antoine has an ally in the woman he has subdued, Aubert likewise finds a convert to his views in the comely servant girl Catherine, who brings him food and tobacco in his distant hiding place and who offers him her virginal warmth and passion: "Yes, I love you. You are alone in me, resplendent like a lamp."

At first Maître Antoine seems successful in his plans, for he has induced the workmen to plug up the spring, drain the lovely pond, and blast with dynamite the majestic oak which shaded the house in summer heat and formed a resting place for innumerable pigeons. As in *Colline*, however, inanimate nature takes her revenge on the man who has violated her. An approching thunderstorm brings night at mid-afternoon, the pigeons fly away in terror, horses break loose in panic from the stable; and Maître Antoine, feverish and delirious, returns home overcome with remorse for the trees he has slaughtered.

In the final act Maître Antoine dies, clinging piteously to the hand of his wife; and Aubert returns to reestablish the old régime of tranquil harmony. The workers calmly smoke their pipes and fish in the pond now restored to its primitive beauty. The triumph of nature is evident in the ironic contrast between the death of Maître Antoine and the joy of Aubert and the workers as they contemplate the shimmering blue trout they have caught in the pond.

The atmosphere of rustic beauty which critics have praised in the play is not merely a poetic setting but also a dramatic force inherent in the action itself, the principle over which the protagonists are fighting. Yet Malherbe has unduly simplified the theme when he sums up: "Maître Antoine and Aubert are two sowers of grain, one with face turned towards the future, the other toward the past. Which one is right?" [1] The conflict is not so much between the forces of progress and the dead hand of the past. It may be questioned whether the greedy efficiency of Maître Antoine with his modern machinery would really contribute to the welfare of this community, for the steep hills are covered with a soil too thin to produce barley and the pond and marshland may well be more productive in fish and sheep than if sowed for wheat. As Villeneuve has so well characterized Antoine: "This intruder is a disintegrating force which threatens a group of landholders. He comes to trouble the rhythm which brought them happiness. He is, in a word, the force of evil which takes on many forms to obstruct the order of nature, and which the ancients . . . sometimes confused with fatality." Giono's message in *Lanceurs de graines* would seem to be not the defense of past tradition against the encroachment of progress but rather man's adaptation to the forces of nature and his realization that beauty of environment is truly as much a reality as sacks of wheat.

There remains a word to say concerning the symbolism of the title, which adds further richness and complexity to the theme. If the struggle for the land has been waged between the two couples, there is another conflict inherent in the play—that between the two sexes. Catherine has come to realize that Aubert's love for her is not all-inclusive, like her need for him, but is shared by his enthusiasm for nature, his preoccupation with creative activity. As Catherine realizes that Maître Antoine on his death bed has lost all desire except for the hand of his wife, she says to the latter: "So Madame, as soon as they no longer have their hand full of grain, no longer can sow grain around them, they become like children and call for our hand to press in theirs." When she asks Madame Delphine if it is not possible for a woman to have this happiness before the approach of death, Antoine's mother consoles her gently: "No, Catherine, sowers of dreams or sowers of wheat, my girl, life has given them the sack of grain and as long as there is life around them they must sow the grain. That is the nature of things."

III   La Femme du boulanger

The last of Giono's three rustic plays was La Femme du boulanger. The reader of Jean le bleu will recall in that volume a fifteen-page episode concerning the flight of the baker's wife with the shepherd of Conches. It has frequently been anthologized and bids fair to become immortal. Giono later enlarged this incident into a three-act drama, performed in 1942 by the Compagnie des Trois Masques in Paris but famous throughout the world in the film version of Marcel Pagnol. For some reason Pagnol gave scant credit to the work of his friend; he merely suggested that the film had been inspired by the short episode in Jean le bleu whereas, according to Villeneuve, he had actually adapted to the screen Giono's three-act drama.

A résumé of the action in the play shows how the original episode, so poignant in its unadorned simplicity, becomes overloaded with philosophical abstraction and dialectical verbosity until we almost lose sight of the abductor and his companion. The opening scenes are excellent for the psychological realism which shows the efforts of the baker to understand the melancholia of his wife, who is roused from her lethargy only by his promise to buy a horse. When the baker learns that his wife has eloped on horseback with the shepherd, he resolves to bake no more for the village and to drown his sorrow in continual libations. The remainder of the act is cluttered up by extraneous characters—three women in black uttering sybilline prophecies, like the witches of Shakespearean drama; three men who make indecent and libidinous remarks; and a young woman who rather brazenly offers to console the baker for the loss of his wife.

In the second act we are transported to the castle of the baron, an amiable, philosophical libertine who is surrounded by his housekeeper, his three "nieces"—in reality mistresses who take regular turns in sharing his couch—his young vicar and his elderly schoolteacher. In an abandoned room of this castle the baker's wife and her lover have been hidden by the "nieces," who are all agog with romantic enthusiasm and mystery. The baker comes to the castle, so inebriated that he believes that not only he but all those he sees about him have died, presumably in a flood from which only the shepherd and his paramour have escaped. (If we may believe Villeneuve, this concept of death by flood represents allegorically the fact that all the community is immersed in egotism and materialism, and love and self-sacrifice have been banished.) The incongruous buffoonery of this scene is enhanced by the willingness of the baron and his entourage to pretend to take this aberration seriously. The baron remarks quizzically: "Though we may not show it, we are really interested in learning how we came to die. . . . You will allow me to sit down, will you not? Even though I am dead, I still have my age to think about."

Desperate over the loss of their daily bread, the villagers have organized a nocturnal hunt of the woods to discover the guilty lovers. Emerging from his intoxication, the baker realizes the ascendancy he has gained and expresses to the baron his desire to be carried in triumphant procession to the church. His glory, the baron assures him, is made manifest by his success in subordinating to his service the two conflicting interests of church and laity when the young priest, attired in borrowed hip boots, takes on his shoulders the elderly schoolmaster in order to cross the marshes and bring back the erring Aurélie. After the tumultuous and lascivious chase of the villagers in the forest, the play once more changes at the end from philosophical marivaudage and boisterous horseplay to poignant realism. The baker, reunited with his wife, offers her the pair of warm stockings he has brought to keep her from catching cold instead of recriminations for her transgressions.

At times the play affords flashes of wit such as the remark: "With all the qualities that a husband demands in his wife, the good Lord could make three female saints." In general, however,

one regrets the absence of a central aim; in this welter of words
and prolixity of personages, the thread of the dramatic story is lost
as the two principal protagonists, the baker and the baron, stand
aloof from the action and exchange metaphysical subtleties.

Despite the attraction which the theater has always exerted for
Giono, his disarming lucidity of self-criticism makes him the first
to recognize that he is not primarily a dramatist. In answer to a
question of Villeneuve, he replied frankly: "The theater requires a
technique and a manner of feeling which I do not possess. I do
not think, for example, that *La Femme du boulanger* could be
performed on a big stage, like the Odéon. The public would be
non-plussed." Giono realized that his drama, primarily one of
ideas, appealed only to a rather select audience; but "the film version pleases the public because the action is moving, because the
village and nature are associated with the action." (He might
have added that the film's success was further enhanced by the
acting of Raimu, one of the great character actors of France.) It is
not surprising that Giono has himself turned to the cinema for his
most recent dramatic productions, *L'Eau vive* and *Crésus*, to be
discussed in a later chapter.

CHAPTER 8

Giono as Epic Novelist

I Le Serpent d'étoiles

AFTER writing the semi-autobiographical *Jean le bleu* and before beginning his trilogy of epic novels, Giono has given us in *Le Serpent d'étoiles* (1933) his own personal impressions of the primitive shepherds who every spring drive their thousands of sheep from the parched plains of lower Provence to the fresh pastures of the Alpine plateaux. The tone is set at the very outset by his quotation from Walt Whitman: "Can your work face the open countryside and the ocean shores?"

In the recital of the shepherd we are reminded of the epic beginning of *Le Grand Troupeau* in its description of the long procession of flocks enveloped in clouds of dust which hide the shepherd from those in front and behind him. If Giono seems obsessed by comparison with water and the sea, it is because the vast herd is in essence liquid and marine: "this flood which scrapes the soil with its belly, its wool, this deep monotonous sound, creates in the shepherd's soul a sense of the sonorous movement and weight of the sea." Giono is successful in achieving a sense of immensity and grandeur in his account of the waves of sheep which form themselves around the helpless dog to crush him and in his portrayal of the mad revolt of the flocks in their vengeance against the shepherd who has imprudently and unjustly struck one of the rams.

The most moving and original episode in the book is the annual meeting of shepherds with their hundred thousand sheep on the lofty, desolate plateau of Mallefougasse, a half-way point on the long trek from the plain to the verdant mountain valleys. Here under the leadership of Le Sarde is performed a spontaneous folk drama, in which Le Sarde is the Narrator and Earth; the other shepherds take the rôles of Sea, River, Mountain, Rain, Cold, Tree, Wind, Grass, Animal, and finally Man. As Peyre has claimed, "if, as he avers, Giono has preserved the original integrity of these folk songs and folk dramas, the book contains some of the most unique documents ever recorded in a popular and spontaneous literature." In a sort of mystic rapture we see evoked here the birth and youth of the world before the final imprint of man. The impression of poetic sorcery is enhanced by the continuous music of æolian harps alternating with flutes and *gargoulettes* (water flutes) and by the haunting magic of the setting which Peyre praises for "a splendor of imagery that recalls the greatest of primitive epics, the *Vedas* and the *Iliad*." The strange title of the book is suggested by the vision of one of the shepherds in whose imagination the night sky represents a great serpent of stars.

In his discussion of Giono's poetic style in *Le Serpent d'étoiles,* Firmin Roz[1] praises the author for his perfect blending of style and content: "For this nature intoxication which no longer makes any distinction between spirit and matter, Giono has succeeded in creating an appropriate style, in which nature and thought mingle and blend all their relationships which become harmonies." One example of Giono's felicity of melody must suffice, and it is taken from his evocation of night, in which so much of this work is enveloped: "At this hour night was complete, dense night whose foliage had never been trimmed, lovely night flapping like a sail, marine night, and its flood rolled over the shore of the trees, in those reefs on the top of the hills; the moon's foam crackled gently against the rocks." Whether Giono speaks of the sun "still perched like a pigeon on the top of our hill" or of the little villages "closed up tight in the evening like surprised turtles," his images are always fresh and original, expressive of his close communion with the world of nature which envelopes and pervades his every fiber. His cosmic imagination has found its wings, and Giono is now ready to embark on his trilogy of epic novels.

II Le Chant du monde (The Song of the World)

As Henri Peyre stated: "Giono was predestined among the French novelists of the century to attempt an epic novel. . . . His humble origins and his obstinate determination to remain a provincial and a man of the people preserved him from the cleverness that gives a veneer of charm, but nothing more, to many brief novels. He had no cynicism and hardly any irony, not even much of a sense of humor, which is a saving grace in some writers but which occasionally paralyzes creation." However inexact this last sentence may seem in its application to the *Chroniques* of Giono today or even to the early Giono of *Naissance de l'Odyssée,* Peyre's statement does characterize aptly his production of the 1930's and explain how it was possible for Giono in the midst of our highly sophisticated age to reproduce in modern guise the spirit of that most ancient of story forms, the epic. Giono has himself defined his aim at this period of his development: "To renew the great Greek tragedies, to revive Pan and the terrestrial mysteries of marvelous paganism, to abstract the soul and substance from everything alive, the clouds, the plain, the wind, the starry sky. . . . And more precisely I wish to speak to you of the eternal verities of the earth and bring you close to joys of such quality that those you already know will fade away as the greatest stars fade when the sun springs up above the mountains."

The reader familiar with Giono's early work will already have glimpsed flashes of epic power in the three short novels comprising the *Trilogie de Pan,* in the opening pages of *Le Grand Troupeau,* and in the festival of shepherds just discussed in *Le Serpent d'étoiles.* Though surpassed perhaps in grandeur and poetic beauty by individual passages in its two successors, *Le Chant du monde* (1934) is universally regarded today as the masterpiece of Giono's epic period. The reason for this esteem is the perfect balance which Giono only here has achieved among pictorial richness, interest and credibility of intrigue, and development of characters which blend into and are explained by their background. With its three divisions representing autumn, winter, and the glorious rebirth of the world in the spring, *Le Chant du monde* possesses at the same time the coherence and unity of great drama and the musical harmonies of a symphony.

The narrative itself is immensely moving in its recital of the expedition of Antonio and Matelot to rescue the latter's son from pursuit by the tyrant Maudru in his mountain domain. It is enveloped, moreover, with epic and cosmic poetry as a result of its unique blending of concrete reality with the sublime grandeur and haunting mystery of its background of the forces of nature. As Marcel Arland has written, "Never in his work have the spirit of the *Odyssey* and that of the Saga been more intimately joined. And the same thing is true for anecdote and legend, man and hero, and finally, men and nature." [2] What gives essential unity to this work is, first of all, the river, with its various moods and seasons. To quote Arland again: "As the *Odyssey* is constructed around the sea, so is *Le Chant du monde* around the River. And the River is present on each page of the book, on which it imposes its current and its meandering, even its seasons; it is the book's soul."

For Giono, the river is a living creature; and he expresses this sense of life and personality in metaphor taken from the animal kingdom: "All day long he has been watching that river ruffling its scales in the sun, then those white horses galloping in the ford with large foamy splashes on their hoofs." As Varillon has so well noted, Giono's style and language are not those of an observer translating the impressions of a spectacle, but of one who is himself immersed in the world of nature he depicts: "Like his hero Antonio, the poet bathes in the river of life. With his hands, his feet, his entire body, he perceives perfumes, colors and sounds like a tissue of relationships more impossible to sever than the universe of Baudelaire." [3]

To this sensibility and subtlety which enable Giono to render palpable the pulsating night of the forest is added an epic grasp which allows him to embrace with poetic sweep an entire horizon: "The night was now turning blue. There was only a reddish star left . . . Day flowed suddenly in a flash along the river, far into the distant water. The mountains lit up. The hills, set abruptly aglowing, started their dance around the fields, and the red sun leapt into the sky, neighing like a stallion." In discussing Giono's rendition of the mystery of the physical universe in *Le Chant du monde*, many critics have used the term "cosmic lyricism." No writer, perhaps, has expressed more forcefully the evolution of the seasons: the dismal rain and fog of autumn, the sparkling radiance of winter frost and snow, the throbbing warmth and exhilaration of the springtime. As Matelot and Antonio plod wearily through the autumnal tempest, Giono adds to the landscape of gloom and despair a touch of cosmic grandeur and terror: "At times, in the surrounding darkness, a strange glimmer kindled northward, and it became impossible to know the time of day. It was like a vision of Doomsday, with everything changed, dawns and sunsets alike, and with the dead rising from their graves." What a contrast later when winter makes of this land a brilliant country which dazzles an eye unprotected by a dark mask: "The sun, scarcely emerging from the horizon and crushed under the weight of relentless azure, would stream all over the frozen snow; the most stunted shrub would blaze up like a flaming heart." And finally after the Odyssey of pursuit in the autumn and the Iliad of murder and revenge in the winter, the rebirth of nature in the spring unfolds the triumphant return of the two sets of lovers towards the peace and tranquility of the South.

Le Chant du monde deserves to be called an epic novel not only because of its grandiose background of natural forces but also because of its characters and narrative. Henri Peyre considers the actors above the common stature of men: "epic heroes not because they accumulate feats in violent battle but because they are the very forces of nature embodied in simple, strong creatures; they echo the song of the world." Peyre makes an exception only of Toussaint, the healer, "the meditative character who always appears among Giono's primitive souls." It is true that Toussaint, like all of Giono's *guérisseurs* or healers, doubtless owes something to the author's memory of his father; Michelfelder thinks he may have come from the pages of Shakespeare. To most readers Toussaint will seem, I think, the most otherworldly and legendary of these protagonists by virtue of the Hugonian contrast of an ugly, misshapen body with a soul of tender compassion, and the likeness to a medieval Merlin with his prophetic fervor and power of divination.

If Antonio, the muscular, sinuous fisherman, is the man of the river, old Matelot, stocky, gnarled, and sturdy, is the true man of the forest. Maudru is presented first as the embodiment of evil who holds the countryside in thrall and whose wrath is like that of an outraged god, but later we see him off his guard as a purely human figure, full of lonely despair over the deaths of his nephew and the woman he had loved. More rugged and epic a character is his sister Gina who fled into the mountain wilderness with three score of her brother's herdsmen and buried one after another a succession of primitive lovers. Her daughter Gina has the same passionate flame within her, and the latter's lover, the red-haired twin, is likewise a creature of adventurous daring and impulse. As a foil for these magnificent and primitive creatures, we have the gently plaintive figure of the blind girl Clara, whose eyes are green like leaves of mint; she also transcends banal reality in her almost mystic power to divine spiritual truth behind the veil of the physical and sensual.

The narrative of *Le Chant du monde* likewise contains many episodes of epic grandeur. As Michelfelder has pointed out, most of these take place in the night when shadows give depth and grandeur to the action portrayed. Among those which hold the reader under a spell, one must mention the following: the orgiastic and mystical celebration of the springtime in the city of Ville-vieille with the dance around the burning figure of the *Mère du Blé;* the lugubrious funeral procession with lanterns which wends its way up the snow-covered mountain to the graveyard where Gina's lovers lie; and the terrible revenge taken by Antonio and the twin when they set the stables of Maudru on fire, releasing into the night the maddened and frenzied bulls. Epic also in their power of fateful presentiment are the image of the white horse always seen on the mountain when a member of the Maudru clan has been slain, and the warning of approaching death which comes to Matelot when the snowcapped mountain seems to him like a great ship of death with all sails set ready to carry him away into the darkness.

III   Que ma joie demeure

Giono tells us that he took the title of *Que ma joie demeure* (1935) from that of Bach's famous chorale, but he omitted the first word, Jesus, "the most important of the entire appeal, the name of the one who is called upon; the only one who up to now has counted for the pursuit of joy." Giono's reason for this omission is his feeling that this word implies a renunciation and, to him, "One must renounce nothing."

Pugnet has called this book the hinge, *le livre-charnière,* of all of Giono's productions because it marks the implicit failure of his apology for peasant life; but Pugnet exaggerates slightly when he says that this is the first work of Giono in which all of the characters are unhappy. (He forgets that one at least, Zulma the simple-minded shepherdess, dressed in fur like the animals she loves, remains untouched by the tragedy of loneliness which weighs so heavily upon the others because of her total absorption in nature.) Another factor which differentiates this novel from the earlier works of Giono, as pointed out by Henri Fluchère[4], is the fact that here for the first time the author is not interested in individual solutions for a couple but in the welfare of an entire social group or community, the inhabitants of the Grémone plateau.

At first glance *Que ma joie demeure* seems much less epic and more realistic than either the preceding or following novel. The narrative, which relates the efforts of Bobi, the wandering acrobat, to bring a sense of joy and beauty to the monotonous and lonesome life of these isolated peasants, is discursive and rambling, filled with the details of husbandry and descriptions of the seasons. The style in the main is simple and free from the exuberant prolixity of imagery of the earlier volumes. Yet, on the whole, in spite of the brooding melancholy which has only temporarily given way to Bobi's poetic magic, the general atmosphere of the book is replete with quiet charm and appreciation of humble things which here are tinged with spiritual beauty. As Peyre has written, "The ardent love of nature, the insight into the life of animals obeying sovereign forces, mating in the woods with a grave delight worthy of Lucretius' avocations, the portraying of the changing seasons and of the work and days of peasant life reminiscent of Hesiod—these are the finest merits of the book." Brasillach likewise, after expressing his distaste for what he calls the detestable Romanticism which pervades the human characters, has only praise for Giono's treatment of animals and of nature: "And enveloping the adventures of the animals, the seasons, nature, wind and storm mingle to enchant us through the simple means of eternal poesy." [5]

One would be justified, therefore, in asking why this novel, which resembles a bucolic idyll, should be included by all critics in the group of epic novels. Part of the answer is given by Henri Fluchère: "In none of his books, even in *Le Chant*, have we yet had that slow and grave ascent which is the trait that marks the epic poet." This critic is referring to the majesty of the central theme, which envelopes and gives unity to the disparate episodes —the gradual diffusion throughout a whole community of the vivifying force represented by Bobi's emphasis upon the beauty of the apparently useless, and the joy of fraternal companionship. According to Michelfelder, this novel is above all the story of man's confrontation with the eternal myths: "The principal myth is that of Dionysus, but the myth of Cybele underlies the entire book, as indeed all his work." The spirit of Dionysus is represented throughout the novel largely by the stag Antoine, who seems more truly alive than some of the human characters. Michelfelder calls this stag "the primitive Dionysus, god of trees and vegetation, god of dampness often represented in the form of a goat, but how much more supple here; a stag is the symbol of the forest and of the beasts of the earth." Brasillach likewise considers the advent of the stag an almost sublime touch, and he is reminded of the most beautiful pages of Kipling—of Mowgli among the wolves of the jungle. Equally magnificent are the other animal episodes in the book; the hunt for the hinds, the bath of the stag in the lake, and especially the magical scene of the lovemaking between the horses which in its quality of myth reminds Brasillach of Virgil and Lucretius, and which Michelfelder calls "the great dance of Dionysus-animal . . . a ride of Centaurs."

Though Giono has stressed the humble, rustic events of daily husbandry, there are at least two episodes in which he has achieved the broad sweep of the epic. The first of these is the rustic banquet, characterized by Peyre as "an epic dinner in which meat and game and fragrant herbs and wine pour out with Rabelaisian lavishness." In this truly Homeric repast, one worthy of the ancient Greeks, we feel as Michelfelder has suggested, the presence of Dionysus, god of intoxication, who makes the entire world dance to the dull rhythm of the blood beating in the veins. Another incident of epic proportions is the harvesting of wheat by the hundreds of mountaineers who have descended on the plains for this annual occasion: "The men of the mountain were singing the great poetic choruses of love and of woman and of the battle against the demons of life. Through the innermost flesh of the city dwellers passed a wind terribly perfumed by the bitter fragrance of blossoms from the almond trees. . . . The voices of the mountaineers were more heavily laden with stars than with night."

In his epic lyricism Giono is especially effective in his sense of the movement of natural forces, such as the wind rolling clouds into fantastic and monstrous images, or the melting of mountain glaciers and snowfields in the spring: "The brooks and torrents sprang up everywhere like sheep racing or cavalcades of plump white mares. High up in the mountains where rested the sharp edges of eternal ice, one could sometimes hear the glaciers neighing; for a moment they would remain motionless, then suddenly with a creaking of their muscles they would rear and the avalanches set free would gallop towards the abyss." No writer, perhaps, has given a more dazzling and terrifying description of lightning than that of the storm in which Bobi meets his death in a flaming vortex of destruction: "The thunderbolt planted a tree of gold between his shoulders." The stark simplicity of this ending forms a fitting climax to the novel. In the light of the descriptive passages quoted, it would be difficult to disagree with Peyre's judgment: "Its magic descriptions unite the splendor of the epic with a familiar simplicity of dialogue that few realistic novels have struck so felicitously."

Why does *Que ma joie demeure* leave a less favorable impression than *Chant du monde* on most readers, even if we agree with the critics who assert that certain scenes and chapters equal anything that Giono has ever written? One may find Brasillach a trifle facetious when he feels "a disrespectful Voltaire rising in us against this new Rousseau trying to make us walk on all fours." Brasillach may be justified in stating that Giono writes better of animals than of men, but he goes too far perhaps when he adds: "He takes away from men the power to reason, he diminishes them, he reduces them to an elementary sensibility, to an instinct of coarseness." It is true that, of all the characters in the novel, only three stand out with any distinction: the mystical and passionate Aurore, the fawn-like shepherdess Zulma, and the poet-acrobat-philosopher Bobi. Indeed, of these, the first two are inarticulate, mystical dreamers; and Bobi himself is far from being thoroughly credible. One has the impression that Giono wavered between making him an abstraction, a mouthpiece for his own generous ideas on poetic beauty and fraternal love, and on the other hand a creature of flesh and blood whose sensuality betrays his lofty ideals.

A second disturbing feature of the book is the apparent inconsistency and cloudiness of philosophy that brought forth almost as many interpretations as there were critics. During the greater part of the novel the author has convinced us that a new awareness of values has permeated this isolated community, bringing hope where there had been despair, a new zest for life and beauty to replace humdrum monotony and brooding care. Then in the last few pages this idyllic dream is rudely shattered by the suicide of Aurore and by the departure of Bobi, accepting the blame remorsefully and shouting "There is no joy." Does this mean, as Pugnet suggests, that Giono suddenly realized the bankruptcy of his philosophy which preached the superiority of rural over urban life, or shall we agree with Fluchère that Giono's conclusion is not really pessimistic but only realistic since the outcome merely shows that Bobi had tried to create his social revolution too rapidly without taking into consideration individual conflicts and weaknesses? Is the collapse of Bobi's dream caused by the tragic flaw in his own character which made him choose the less worthy of the two women who loved him, or was his dream unrealizable in any case, as Pugnet suggests, because "the poet's joy cannot be shared. Bobi feels that he cannot share his joy and that there is no joy for a poet if he does not share it."

It is not easy to see clearly among the conflicting interpretations. For one thing, why need we assume that with Bobi's departure all his teachings must perish? The group still has its newly awakened appreciation of beauty in flower and foliage, its reborn joy in working and sharing together. That this novel marks the end of Giono's optimistic solutions cannot be denied, however; for in his later works one no longer finds the happy endings of his earlier volumes. When questioned about the three suicides in the story, particularly that of Aurore which seems to clash melodramatically and almost crudely with the gentle tenor of the narrative, Giono replied that the blazing sun and unflecked sky produce such loneliness among the isolated dwellers on Lure Mountain that this district has the highest percentage of suicides in France. When asked whether the dénouement meant that his outlook on life had become more pessimistic, he answered, however, that this was far from the truth; he had merely come to realize that it is possible to bring happiness only to individuals and not to an entire group.

IV Batailles dans la montagne

Batailles dans la montagne (1937) is the most ambitious, the most truly epic of the novels in this cycle. One must agree with Peyre when he writes: "The story leaps almost beyond human bounds; the actors are hardly made real. . . . Giono's epic qualities have swollen dangerously." According to Villeneuve, who had access to Giono's unpublished diary: "No work was to require of him more effort or procure him such feelings of emotion." For more than a year he remained steeped in its creation, even to the extent of forgetting for days on end to eat or shave. To one who knows Giono, however, it is difficult to believe that he abandoned his pipe for two whole days. Apparently Giono no longer regards this book as one of his better volumes, for his biographer Chonez quotes him as saying: "I wanted to employ a muddy style to paint mud—the result is unreadable."

As in the case of *Que ma joie demeure*, *Batailles* aroused tremendous controversy among critics. Some of those who agreed with Giono's own later harsh judgment are Firmin Roz[6] who considered it difficult to read because of its minute, compressed and sometimes strange detail, and Henri Peyre who charges that "the dramatic and even the plain human quality of Giono's earlier work seems gone." On the other hand, Henri Pourrat[7] considers *Batailles* the finest of Giono's works, and Henri Bidou calls it a magnificent book: "Never has the epic genius of M. Giono painted with greater power the forces of nature and the combats of man against those gods as much alive as in the primeval days of the world." [8] Occupying a middle ground between these two extremes of denigration and hyperbole are Jacques Madaule and Robert Brasillach. The former, although he criticizes the ensemble for leaving the reader confused and disconcerted, nevertheless is full of praise for individual episodes such as the epic combat of the hero Saint-Jean against the frenzied bull.[9] The latter, while admitting that "M. Giono becomes at times a whirling dervish whom we watch without being able to share his delirium," is impressed nonetheless by the potential beauty of the book which, if the author had consented to be a little more intelligible, might have made him "the true rival of Vergil and Mistral in the French language." [10]

The action of this novel concerns the efforts of a mountain village to escape a gigantic flood caused by the melting of a glacier and the obstruction of the river by a landslide. Never, perhaps, has Giono exceeded the intensity of hallucinating emotion created by such episodes as the conquest of the murderous bull, the procurement of the dynamite, and the final expedition to explode the dam which had caused the inundation. The setting likewise is grandiose and awe inspiring. Starting, as always, with a basis of realistic observation—in this case, a grotto which he had observed on the mountain at Tréménis overlooking the plain with its four hamlets and five small streams—Giono has enlarged this scene to form the vast gray mass of the glacier La Treille, whose massive outline casts a shadow of foreboding over the immense landscape.

We have seen that *Chant du monde* has been likened to an

Iliad and *Odyssey,* and *Que ma joie demeure* to the myth of Dionysus and Cybele. As for *Batailles,* Michelfelder, preoccupied as always with the classical inspiration of Giono, cannot refrain from comparing the episode of Saint-Jean in quest of the dynamite with that of Prometheus going to the isle of Lemnos to seize the divine torch from Hephaestos.[11] Yet most critics have found in *Batailles* a predominantly biblical rather than classical foundation. This basis is manifest in part in the character of Bourrache, a sort of prophet from the Old Testament, who is constantly reminding the peasants that their misfortune is a visitation from Jehovah to punish them for their godlessness. It may be wondered, however, whether Bourrache is not in the eyes of Giono a satiric figure, sadistic, bristling with self-importance and over-weaning smugness. More truly a biblical character is the wealthy and majestic Boromée, who, like a patriarch in the Old Testament, has twenty-eight wives and thirty-seven children. When Sarah arrives at his home as a servant and becomes his common-law wife during the first evening, the critic Brasillach is reminded of Ishmael, and Bidou of the Moabite. At times, moreover, the language of the book has a definitely biblical flavor, as in the description of the transformation which takes place on the mountainside as the soil becomes fluid from the seeping of the glacier: "The forests bend towards the earth. The water smokes along the rocks. The meadows flow like fountains." Finally the vastness of the inundation which has brought disaster to thirty cantons reminds the reader of the biblical flood—and the knoll of Villard l'Eglise which shelters the survivors and their livestock plays the same rôle as the ark.

Yet the essentially epic quality of this book is found in the character of its hero Saint-Jean, who, in Peyre's words, is "more a symbol than a living man; Jacob wrestling with the angel or Prometheus defying the gods to serve man . . . his epic stature alone fills the novel." Though Saint-Jean seems human enough at first in his humble calling as a carpenter, in his brotherly affection for his group and particularly for his comrade Antoine, and in his bashful, almost inarticulate love for Sarah, he lifts himself under the spur of catastrophe to superhuman heights of endurance, courage, and selflessness. One must agree with Michelfelder's statement: "In the extraordinary efforts he has to accomplish, Saint-Jean loses his human stature; he becomes as strong and powerful as the dynamite which he warms against his breast." And Madaule terms him "almost as much a myth as the glacier of La Treille."

In summary, it may be said that *Batailles* marks the extreme limit of Giono's epic inspiration. He realized that he had exhausted this poetic vein, for this is the last novel of what has been called his first manner. This novel is followed by the very different style of the *Chroniques,* in which the lyric rhapsodies of nature are subordinated to a sobriety of expression almost metallic in its hardness, even though his fondness for strange, mysterious adventures still persists.

V *Summary*

In comparing the three novels, one may say that *Batailles* has the greatest sweep, the most impressive grandeur of natural setting, and the most dramatic theme—the struggle for survival against the forces of nature. By judicious cutting, particularly in the confused and prolix introduction, this somewhat disorganized and disconcerting work might have become the finest of the three. *Que ma joie demeure,* less compelling in its story, though full of admirable scenes and descriptions which could be chosen for an anthology, is too episodic in narrative and too contradictory in theme to be entirely satisfactory. On the other hand, *Chant du monde* because of the perfect equilibrium of Giono's epic qualities —grandeur of natural beauty, credibility and interest of narration, and perfect blending of heroic characters with their background —will remain for most readers, and I believe for Giono himself, his true masterpiece in the epic novel. We may even, like Marcel Arland, prefer it to everything else Giono has written:

Just as the great Hugo, the authentic one, is not the modest and plaintive author of *Feuilles d'Automne* but the visionary of the *Légende des Siècles* and of *Satan,* so it is by neglecting almost every care for verisimilitude that Giono proceeds to give his measure, build his world and sometimes convince us of its truth. These mountains and forests, these rivers and glaciers, these dawns and shadows are the true personages of Giono; their mere presence is already speech, or rather song, a tragic hymn.

CHAPTER 9

The Messiah of Contadour

I *Travel*

IN 1931 Giono was sent by the French Service of Propaganda to give lectures in Berlin. To his amazement, he was greeted at the station by students singing verses of Mistral in Provençal. After speaking to an enthusiastic audience of fifteen hundred in the great hall, he disregarded warnings not to go into the workers' quarter of the east side for fear of possible hostility, talked of Verdun days with a German veteran he met in a tavern, and soon found himself the center of an admiring group. According to Villeneuve, Jean Giraudoux, who happened to be in Berlin at this time, was much amused by these friendly meetings; but both he and Giono felt, like Victor Hugo a hundred years before, that only a Franco-German understanding could assure the equilibrium of Europe.

Since Giono had resigned his position in the bank, his custom was to spend the summer months in the Alps. During Aline's childhood, the family stayed at Saint-Julien-Beauchêne and, while Sylvie was a baby, in the vicinity of Briançon: "To see mountains in front of me has always filled me with a feeling of excitement. I have observed also that there are fewer imbeciles at an altitude of three thousand meters than at sea level."

In *Voyage en Italie* we have a charming description of one of these summers, that of 1934 spent at Embrun where Giono had rented four large rooms in a convent-like house facing the ramparts and gates of Briançon. Below, the murmur of the Clarée River as it merged with the Durance lulled the family to sleep at night with the sound of its rushing current. An orchard surrounded with walls gave the house its similarity to a monastery, so dear to the heart of Giono. "Just before dawn the poplar trees would begin to rustle more loudly than the torrents, in the wind from the Lauteret." Every morning was begun by listening to Bach's Brandenburg Concertos on the phonograph. With Lucien

Jacques, who was living with them, Giono formed the habit of going into the meadows to gather pink mushrooms; "and we ate so many that we had many disturbing hallucinations which came over us while we were wide awake." While Giono worked in the somber, sonorous attic, Aline made friends with the worms, scarabs, and the birds in the orchard; and Sylvie grew plump and beautiful in her cradle.

II *Origin, Development of Contadour*

Katherine Clarke states that, after the publication of *Que ma joie demeure* in 1935, Giono received hundreds of passionate letters from young people all over Europe who called on him to help them realize their dreams of peace and fraternal happiness. "We too want to live," they cried; "tell us how we must go about it. How can we, enslaved as we are to technology, find a lasting joy?" In the wake of Gide, a fervent admirer of Giono ever since the publication of *Colline,* there followed a procession of distinguished writers to his home—among them were Saint-Exupéry, Dabit, Barbusse, Jean Paulhan, Marcel Arland and the American Henry Miller. Hundreds of unknown youths came also—students, workers, and artists from many foreign countries as well as France. "Every day they arrived in greater numbers," wrote Pugnet

and during Easter vacation or in the summer in groups and caravans. Manosque was becoming a goal of pilgrimage. With his accustomed kindness Giono allowed everyone to climb up to his "lighthouse." They piled up on the divan, on the floor, they touched the pipes, the Negro mask, the books. He would listen to everyone with patience; they called him Jean. Then Giono would start to read the last page he had written or tell a story. There were also long musical—tobacco evenings around the phonograph of the house. Some one would put on the Symphonies and the Brandenburg Concertos, very often the variations of Goldberg.

There came a time when many had to wait in the stairway, the garden, the kitchen and even stand in line before the door. "There are too many of them," Mme Giono said at last. "This can't go on; you ought to take them for a walk." On the morning of September 1, 1935, Giono set out therefore with some forty of the faithful, knapsacks on their backs, in the direction of the mountain of Lure which had fascinated him since his early childhood. On the way they stopped at farms to eat with the peasants and to sleep in barns. They passed through Banon and the abandoned village of Redortiers (the Aubignane of *Regain*) on the arid, wind-swept plateau of Contadour, some five thousand feet above sea level where a few sheep were browsing on the stunted grass amidst clumps of wild lavender. Here Giono sprained his knee, and the caravan decided to halt near the tiny hamlet of Contadour.

So attracted were they by the spacious solitude and by the hospitality of Mme Merle that they later bought a hectare of land and erected a dwelling and sheepfold. For the time being, they lived in a barn in which lavender was distilled. "We cooked on a great black fireplace," Giono relates in *Les Vraies Richesses,* "all greasy from the soot full of resin from the branches of pines. We ate a lamb we had bought from the shepherds. Towards evening Mme Merle, the queen of this wild country, would come by the winding road among the chestnut trees. She would sit down with us and partake of that joy she heard bubbling forth on the plateau like the foam from a newly opened spring." After dinner they gathered around the blazing hearth to hear Giono tell stories "about the stars, the great legends, the mingling of man and the world."

The first Contadour was followed by many others during the next six years, the second taking place at Easter, 1936. In Giono's diary for the fifth of May of that year may be read this notation: "We made the doors and windows of the house. Lots of visitors for Easter. Lucien Jacques made the fresco. Excellent organization of the library." On August 30 he wrote: "Tomorrow Lucien and I set out for the third Contadour. Joy to receive such dear friends." And, on September 24: "The third Contadour was admirable. Exceeded the most optimistic expectations." According to Romée de Villeneuve, Giono's purpose on these expeditions was "to form an élite, to make them love nature and countryfolk, to render them conscious of European solidarity, to remove them or cure them from deadly ideologies."

A more definite purpose, however, seems to have been the use of Contadour as a sort of *banc d'essai,* or proving ground, to test the aptitude of those who wished to return and establish themselves upon the land, as a result of the movement known as *Les Auberges de la Jeunesse* (Youth Hostels). In an interview given to Edmond Epardaud by Mme Reyne, keeper with her husband of the Manosque *auberge,* she stated: "M. Giono won't tell you all we owe to his intelligence and kindness. We have been able to settle young people, couples from the city, in various corners of the country. They have all stayed. They are living there the life of the peasants and are adapting themselves to the soil. Farms are going to be created to sustain the effort of the *auberges.*" [1]

For the internal rule of Contadour, a Constitution was drawn up to represent the high ideals of comradeship and mutual understanding which were to animate the group. Yet as Fernand Vial [2] has pointed out in his interesting essay on Giono, these neophytes possessed a saving sense of humor which prevented them from taking themselves too seriously. If Article III states solemnly "Only sincere people, free from all personal interest, are admitted to Contadour," Article VI continues: "No newspaper may cross the threshold of Contadour" and Article XI ordains with tongue in cheek: "Every political, religious and culinary opinion is allowed at Contadour, but the greatest tolerance is expected from all the members."

III *Unfriendly Critics*

As was only to be expected, some rather caustic remarks have been made in derision of the nature-worshippers who followed their *cher maître* to his mountain shrine. Ernst Eric Noth,[3] for instance, was a little shocked by the tendency to call their leader Jean-le-Bleu or even Jean-le-Magnifique, and by the suggestion among some of the faithful that they really ought to proceed from the railway station to Giono's house on hands and knees. Michel Ragon likewise stresses the shallow insincerity of some of these campfollowers: "One could see at the Contadour society people, thinking they had become peasants, going to fetch water in luxurious automobiles." Even Pugnet, feeling no doubt that his sarcasm has been authorized by Giono's later disillusionment with the movement, chortles with amusement:

The Contadour became the place for the devotees of Gionoism. One found all sorts of people there, many young men, but also old anarchists, old maids in shorts and brogans come to refresh themselves in the flowers of the fields, couples of young workers, post-graduates in all disciplines and the simple minded. Sometimes even playboys, after a night of spree or gambling at Aix or Monte Carlo would arrive at the sacred spot. It was generally at dawn, which is one of the moments when one desires to be pure. They would hide their car behind some hedge, untie their cravat and roll the trousers of their Prince Albert up to the thigh. Automatically they would be thrown into the sheepfold, where there was at least a half-meter of dung; they would find also a phonograph and the Pastoral Symphony.

IV Les Cahiers

Like those earlier experiments in communal living, the rustic Brook Farm of the New England Transcendentalists and the Abbaye de Créteil of Duhamel, Vildrac and Company, the bucolic charm of the Contadour had its echo in print. A quarterly called *Les Cahiers du Contadour* was published in twenty numbers under the joint editorship of Giono and his friend Lucien Jacques. A preliminary article suggests the scope and spirit of this publication: "I don't mean to say that we are going to speak of Contadour as apostles; I mean to say that in the purity of our hearts we are going to express our joy and pride. Contadour was born out of our joy." Other articles of the *Cahiers* have such lyrical titles as "Promises of Contadour," "The Promised Land," and "Peace at Contadour."

In addition to Giono's own contributions, which include prose poems, unpublished chapters of *Le Grand Troupeau* and his play *Le Bout de la route,* there were poems and engravings by Lucien Jacques, poems by Charles Vildrac and Romain Rolland, excerpts from the war memories of the philosopher Alain; and in translation poems by Siegfried Sassoon, O'Neill's *Mourning Becomes Electra,* and Melville's *Moby Dick.*

Giono is today his own most severe critic of this enterprise which he tends to deprecate and minimize. A few years ago he expressed his disillusionment to Claudine Chonez:

The earlier message (note that I do not like the word message) was already out of date. I wanted to make known that joy which is possible in the life of poor peasants thanks to the total absence of "false riches." There was also the influence of the war in Spain. (One must have communist sympathies at the age of twenty, otherwise one is idiotic or hard-hearted. Afterwards comes disenchantment.)

It was a source of misunderstandings. My young people were seeking universal formulas, which they expected me to give. And I said to them: "One creates one's happiness by himself. Each must find his own solution." They at once placed themselves upon a social plane, and I on a romantic, passionate one, a little utopian perhaps. My teaching has been grossly exaggerated. It amounted to nothing more than ballads, camping and the salami sausage eaten together. But many took themselves terribly seriously. *The Cahiers?* That was chiefly to please them.

CHAPTER 10

Three Books of Social Propaganda

I Their Similarity

THE remark just quoted represents the sober and disillusioned view of Giono today concerning his campaign to reform society. It is obviously a far cry, however, from his attitude at the time of the Contadour for he was to publish in the next six or seven years a trilogy of major propaganda works—*Les Vraies Richesses, Le Poids du ciel,* and *Triomphe de la vie*—in addition to three minor writings—*Lettre aux paysans, Refus d'obéissance,* and *Précisions.* Giono's penchant for the trilogy form incidentally is rather striking. Besides the two series just mentioned, we have had the three rustic novels; three epics; and, since World War II, three novels in which Angelo is the chief protagonist and three which center about Pauline, Marquise de Théus.

Before analyzing in detail the three major works of social theory, it might be advisable to consider first their similarity of style and viewpoint. An anonymous critic found *Les Vraies Richesses* difficult to classify—"neither a novel nor a nouvelle, and not an essay either; rather an informal meditation, a passionate monologue, an ardent appeal." This description applies with equal felicity to the other two works, for they have in common a glorification of the simple life as opposed to the mechanical servitude of modern society, expressed in flamboyant lyrical outbursts and cosmic abstractions alternating with passages of poignant and restrained realism. In all three volumes the somewhat banal and reactionary thesis of the polemist is redeemed at times by the rich visual imagery of the poet.

II Les Vraies Richesses

In the Preface to *Les Vraies Richesses* (1936), Giono explains that this book is the answer to his comrades of Contadour who had questioned him concerning joy. He begins with a fascinating picture of a worker's quarter in Paris near the humble little hotel, on rue du Dragon, where Giono was accustomed to stay on his infrequent visits to the capital. This populous section comes alive before our eyes with all the realism of a Teniers painting, as Giono shows us the tradespeople bustling to and fro, eating and drinking in their *bistros*, occupied with their daily tasks. As a comrade and friend, he would like to speak to them of the joys of creative work, of the glories of nature in the countryside; but, denatured and desiccated by their grim struggle for existence and by the grinding monotony of the machine age, they are unable to hear his message. What impresses the author above all in this great metropolis is its solitude: "But it is a solitude which is not harmony and divine concert, but rather the total silence of the soul caused by suffocation." Giono sees the city helpless under the implacable law of the machine: "An endless chain of slavery in which everything is destroyed without creating either joy or liberty."

In contrast with this picture of futility and servitude is the central episode of the book, the lighting of the communal bake oven in the mountain hamlet of Trièves, where forty men and women gather in fraternal comradeship to enjoy the fruit of their labor, the savory fragrance of freshly baked bread. In this connection, Katherine Clarke has pointed out the importance of this lyric symbol in Giono's work: "It is this which crowns the work of the whole year and becomes the symbol of the simplicity, beauty and grandeur of life. Because for the poet bread takes on a biblical importance, such as we find in the Lord's Prayer, in the words of Christ." This episode furnishes Giono also the occasion to contrast the independence of the peasants with the commercial greed of speculators who burn or denature wheat in order to raise the market price and with others who slaughter little pigs in Illinois (doubtless an allusion to President Roosevelt's New Deal) while a large part of the world goes naked and hungry.

"For man's riches are in his heart. It is in his heart that he is king of the world. To live does not demand possession of so many things." This statement is the heart of Giono's message in *Les Vraies Richesses*, and we are reminded of the parallel with the early Duhamel—"If civilisation is not in the heart of man, it is nowhere" (*Civilisation*), and of the latter's lyrical *Possession du monde* and of his bitter excoriation of American slaughterhouses in *Scènes de la vie future;* like a twentieth-century Rousseau, Giono calls us back to the simple life: "The things of which thou art deprived are winds, rains, snows, suns, mountains, rivers, forests: the true riches of man." Yet it would not be fair to assume that Giono limits himself to purely sensuous rhapsodies, for he is careful to make room in his assemblage of peasants and artisans for the creator of spiritual joys—the musician and the poet. In his picture of the philosophy student working in the quarries, reading Plato and Virgil in his moments of leisure and setting out on Sundays to seek mushrooms in the forest, a volume of Shakespeare in his knapsack, Giono emphasizes the value of knowledge not for utilitarian pursuits but as "une noblesse intérieure" which can deepen and enrich the understanding of nature.

It is a facile exercise for the critics of this work to imitate the scornful remark of Voltaire about Rousseau whom he accused of wishing to make us "walk on all fours"—and few indeed have resisted the temptation. Thus André Thérive, calling Giono "a laïcized Claudel, a southern Maeterlinck," summarizes his essential doctrine as: "Don't be intelligent (as if this danger threatened our country)." [1] If Giono should be successful in restoring primitivism to the land, Thérive thinks it probable that, rather than restoring the age of Saturn, the new era would be drowned in violence and bloodshed. "It is an absurd postulate to imagine bipeds capable of browsing on grass like peaceful animals and reconstructing Eden by the mere profession of their fundamental innocence." Another critic wonders if Giono really believes that by razing cities, burning libraries and hospitals, breaking civic bonds and reducing the complexities of society by force he could make the modern world a sort of immense Tahiti, a primitive Eden in which happiness would be distributed to all; and he reproaches Giono bitterly for not offering a more practical succor for suffering humanity.[2] Still another anonymous writer, while placing Giono in the first rank of his generation between Montherlant and Chamson, nevertheless takes him to task for the exaggerations and confusion of his generous thought, pointing out that not all who have deserted the country have done so from greed, but rather from economic necessity. "M. Giono's appeal will only give city dwellers a more bitter realization of their servitude."

François Varillon is perhaps the only critic of stature to find merit in *Les Vraies Richesses*. Pointing out that Giono is following in the footsteps of Ruskin, Vigny, Rousseau, and the Bible (Jeremiah XXXV) in his diatribes against mechanization, urban life, and progress, Varillon warns us not to smile at this book as merely the revery of a visionary, for Giono's cry of protest and alarm deserves to be heard. "True riches are there—this resistance to growing old, this respect for beautiful materials and beautiful craft, this cult of fraternal labor, this profound feeling for the necessity of art and play in civilisation, this need for nimbleness and mirth in work, this solicitude for poverty, this generosity." [3] Yet even Varillon feels that all these are not *the* true riches; he finds an element of danger in Giono's doctrine because it makes so little distinction between men and animals, writes God with a small letter, and places undue stress on mere instinct.

III   Le Poids du ciel

The chief difference between *Le Poids du ciel* (1938) and its predecessor is the change of emphasis from the purely social to the political plane and the aggressive denunciation by Giono of all political parties in Europe (including the army) which enrolled men under political banners and deprived them of their independence as free souls. The steps in the evolution of Giono's political beliefs will be discussed in some detail in the following chapter. Suffice it to say that, by the publication of *Le Poids du ciel*, this evolution was completed; Giono had freed himself from the shackles of any formal organization or ideology, in particular that of the Communists.

After an hallucinating and vertiginous opening chapter called *La Danse des Ames* which paints a terrifying picture of the future —one reminiscent of Orwell's *1984*—in which we see modern souls leaving human bodies, becoming metallic skeletons and Bessemer furnaces, the remainder of the book, more sober and restrained in language than is usual with Giono at this period, is a plea for the grandeur and beauty of the free man. To attain this goal, Giono rejects without compromise all the bases of modern industrial society, beginning with all systems of government; for "no political régime has been able in a thousand years to give the thousandth part of happiness afforded by one night's sleep." One is reminded of passages in Saint-Exupéry's *Citadelle* attacking dictatorship either by the crowd or by Fascist chiefs when one reads: "I am the enemy of the party, whatever it may be. The mass-man, on which so many intellectuals insist, does not exist. What does exist is the one who commands the mass, who dictates to the mass." All parties, according to Giono, have used the same outworn shibboleths—happiness of humanity, liberty, bread, fatherland, grandeur of the individual, liberation of the working class, and the like—without ever having solved any problem. As for the leaders of the day, Lenin, Stalin, Hitler, and Mussolini, history has swallowed up dozens of their ilk without a trace. All political systems are only tissues of lies which abolish individual liberty.

Without realizing the significance, perhaps, of what he is about to say, Giono admits, however, that nothing which he has just expressed could be printed or even written on paper in Germany, Italy, or Russia. He adds that he could not even say these things aloud, even think them, for fear that they might show upon his face. Strange indeed that Giono did not realize that this fact alone was enough to invalidate his equivalence of all social systems, for herein lies the essential difference between the free democracies of the West and the slavery of totalitarian régimes.

Giono's uncompromising pacifism, which lies at the basis of his opposition to contemporary society, is often apparent in *Le Poids du ciel,* as in his denunciation of slogans of nationalism and patriotic heroism. "The true grandeur of man has nothing to do with nation or class, but only with the individual; and all the elements of this grandeur are found in work within the compass of man and the reach of his hands." He contrasts peasant society, which can exist only on peace, with an industrial society that lives better on war than on peace and "soon will be able to live only on war."

If Giono detests capitalism primarily because he thinks it always leads to war, he is quick to add that it is not capitalism but the factory which debases man. He has no patience with those who would destroy capitalism but keep the factory, for doing so would only create State Capitalism and the worker would still be chained to his machine: "This would not have cured the sole chief malady of modern times, the malady of the individual." For Giono the machine is the ogre which today has denatured the worker's soul. To those who claim that the machine has lightened man's labor, Giono replies: "Technology removes the diversity of men's work, it takes away the problem, it abolishes the pleasure. It transforms work into a task; it increases the inner unhappiness of men who are forced into tasks presenting no possibility of interest or of joy." How different is the artisan, proud of his skill and craft, from the worker bound to his machine. Akin to the peasant, self-sufficient on his little farm, is the artisan, creative and independent of spirit.

It is interesting to note that French critics have been much more favorable to *Le Poids du ciel* than to *Les Vraies Richesses*, despite the more iconoclastic tone of the former. Giono's harshest critic, André Thérive, for instance, though still critical of Giono's exuberant style, admires the noble and striking picture of rustic customs in the last chapter. Robert Kemp is delighted with Giono's condemnation of the mass, glorification of the individual, and scorn for all political parties: "M. Giono seems to me to have become quite wise. And some other intellectuals appear to be on the point of listening to him." [4] Max Brunher, after some restrictions against Giono's tendency to subordinate his poetic gifts to preaching, concluded that "his work is a song of hope, a hymn to the courage of peaceful man and to life." [5] Even a clerical commentator, after reproaching Giono for his militant atheism, praised him for his occasional good sense as evidenced in the statement that "there is no grandeur except in the individual and in liberty." [6] Yet almost all critics have been nettled by the closing lines of the volume: "I make no effort either to be liked or followed. I detest being a follower and I have no esteem for those who follow me. I write so that each one may make his own reckoning." Perhaps the most indulgent reaction to this surly and insincere *boutade* is that of Jacques Madaule: "Giono's case is singular and pathetic. He is a prophet who does not believe in God and who doesn't want anyone to believe in him." [7]

IV Triomphe de la vie

When *Triomphe de la vie* (1942) was published during the Occupation, Giono stated its purpose as follows: "It is a complement to *Les Vraies Richesses* in which I had given a vision of peasant society. I had neglected to develop a very important side of the society: that of the artisan." As will be seen in a later chapter, this book was used by some of the Resistance writers after the war to prove that Giono had allied himself with Marshal Pétain's reactionary campaign for French agriculture and industry. Though the book is dated January-July, 1941, the ideas expressed, in their glorification of rural joys, are only an amplification of those to be found in his earlier social treatises.

As for the choice of the title, it seems to have been inspired by Giono's reaction against the famous painting of Breughel entitled "The Triumph of Death." Just as George Sand in revulsion against Albrecht Dürer's ghastly reproduction of Death stalking the countryside had decided in *La Mare au diable* to show a truer picture of rustic life, so Giono, abandoning the polemic tone of *Le Poids du ciel*, endeavors in this final volume of his social trilogy to show the felicity and the *joie de vivre* existing in the fraternal cooperation between artisans and peasants. If the style here possesses more unity than in the previous volumes, it is perhaps because Giono frankly admits: "I am not a distinguished economist nor a politician; I am only a poet."

Though *Triomphe de la vie* is presented as a series of rambling reflections which came to the author as he was sitting in a café in Marseilles, they may be divided into three fairly distinct parts. The first describes communal life in an idyllic little Alpine village such as Mens, with its interdependence among the farmers and the various artisans who supply their daily wants—harness maker, weaver, mason, wheelwright, cabinetmaker, cobbler, and baker. Yet, if his villagers need the material products created by these artisans, they thirst equally for those intangible blessings which can be furnished only by the poet and musician: "What the community lacks in order to be complete is the one who will furnish the materials for this creation through the heart. This is what I call a poet."

The most eloquent pages which Giono devotes to the praise of the artisan describe, with both realistic detail and lyric fervor, the artistry of the shoemaker. Brasillach reminds us in this connection of the words of Rodin who compared the trade of cobbler to that of sculptor.[8] It is obvious that Giono has in mind the heroic, almost legendary figure of his father to whom he pays a filial tribute here, quoted in an earlier chapter, as warmly moving as that in *Jean le bleu*.

The middle section of *Triomphe* is devoted to an idyllic picture of a peasant fête at the patriarchal farm of Silence, in which the sensual delights of the table and the joyous animation of dance and music are enhanced by the poetic setting of encircling mountains.

The volume closes with the scenario for a possible movie which forms a sequel to Giono's early novel *Regain*. The three families living on the desolate plateau of Aubignane, finding the soil too obdurate for ordinary commercial plows, send Gaubert, son of the former blacksmith, into the valley to persuade Augustin, an elderly blacksmith who has been retired by the railway, to join their little community and to create for them the special type of plow which can render their soil more productive. Perhaps it will be possible to solve two problems at the same time, for one of the families has a daughter of twenty-six who seems destined for lonely spinsterhood in the absence of marriageable bachelors. The project is successful; the smoke from the reactivated smithy gives new life to the little village; and Eugénie, dazzled by the artistic skill of the old blacksmith, shows herself willing to join her fortunes with his. We are left therefore with the optimistic feeling that life in Aubignane will continue victorious.

V *Evaluation*

It is obvious enough today that his period of social propaganda is the weakest part of Giono's work, the one least likely to survive. While there are many individual passages of great poetic beauty, particularly in the realistic pictures of communal life among French peasants and artisans in Alpine villages, there is little in these books which has not been better expressed in Giono's rustic novels. To restrain Giono's innate tendency toward verbosity and proliferation it would seem that the framework of a dramatic story is needed. Yet if Giono today, disillusioned perhaps by his two imprisonments during the war and conscious of his inability to bring happiness to large groups, has definitely withdrawn from "la littérature engagée" in preference to sober, pessimistic stories with historical background, it is interesting to recall this generous if utopian period in which he was the idol of revolutionary youth in Europe. There is, moreover, one aspect of this early enthusiasm which still burns brightly in the elderly writer today: his unshakeable pacifism. And though it was hardly necessary for Giono to confess that he was neither an economist nor a political scientist but only a poet, it is nevertheless noteworthy that, long before Gide, he succeeded in perceiving the myth of Communist pretentions for ushering in the millennium of social justice and liberty.

CHAPTER 11

Pacifism and First Imprisonment

I *Flirtation with Communism*

THE reader will recall that Giono's ardent denunciation of war had its first literary manifestation in his novel *Le Grand Troupeau* (1931) and in his semi-autobiographical *Jean le bleu* (1932). The basis for this feeling was not the non-resistance of a Gandhi but rather his passionate grieving for the loss of Louis David and his sense of futility in the sacrifices which the war entailed:

Ah, if it were a question of defending rivers, hills, mountains, skies, winds, rains, I would say, "Willingly, that is our job; let us fight, all our happiness in life is there." No, we have defended the sham name of all that. As for me, when I see a river, I say "river" when I see a tree, I say "tree"; I never say "France." That does not exist. Ah, how willingly I would give away that false name that one single one of those dead, the simplest, the most humble, might live again! Nothing can be put into the scales with the human heart . . . There is no glory in being French. There is only one glory; in being alive.

We may feel that Giono's choice of words here is unfortunate, but we cannot doubt the sincerity of the anguish from which they sprang.

It was doubtless the preoccupation of Communism with anti-war activity that brought about Giono's brief flirtation with this ideology. Under the leadership of Vaillant-Couturier, the leading French Communist journalist of the day, the Association des Ecrivains et des Artistes Révolutionnaires, popularly known as the *AEAR*, was organized in 1931. The purpose of this group, according to Professor B. R. Jordan of Duke University who has made a detailed study of Communist activity in French literature before and after World War II, was to bring the creative artists into more effective contact with the masses: "In 1934 the project was further implemented by the formation of sectional *Maisons de*

Culture, which were to be centers for lectures, concerts and the like. This savors of the Universités Populaires of the turn of the century." It was in 1934 that Giono, in a letter to the editor of *Commune* (January-February, 1934), stated the case for many of the collaborators: "Up to now I have struggled passionately against war. I was wrong to believe I could do so outside the parties through my own individual action. I know now that it can be attained only in the political domain. War cannot be separated from the bourgeois State. It is after reaching this decision that I made up my mind to adhere to the *AEAR.*"

Giono wrote several articles for Communist-oriented magazines such as *L'Europe* and *Vendredi* (which latter published Chapter V of *Les Vraies Richesses* and in 1937 the Preface to his *Refus d'obeissance*); he later refused further collaboration with *Vendredi* which he found too sympathetic with Bolshevist ideology. Already in 1934, in spite of the pleadings of Gide and Malraux and overtures from the Committee of Soviet Writers, Giono had refused to attend a congress of leftist writers in Moscow. The chief reason for his increasing disillusionment with the Communist sympathizers seems to have been that the Communist Party, originally the advocate of peace as opposed to Fascist sword-rattlers, had now begun to preach intervention against the Italians in Ethiopia, Franco in Spain, and Hitler in Austria and later Czechoslovakia. The definite decision of Giono to break with his former friends may be dated from this entry in his Journal of November 20, 1936: "Persuaded now that it is necessary to reject fascism, nazism and communism. Among them it is only a struggle among dictators . . . I believe that I am violently that non-conformist of which Gide speaks, even more than he."

II *Pacifist Endeavors*

From this moment to the outbreak of World War II Giono was preoccupied with the growing tyranny of the three dictators —Mussolini, Hitler, and Stalin—and with the conviction that Europe was being led inexorably to the precipice of war. In 1937 he published *Refus d'obeissance* consisting of two parts; an article against war written for the magazine *Europe* in 1934, and four unpublished chapters of his *Le Grand Troupeau.* In the former Giono states: "Twenty years have gone by. And in twenty years, despite life with its sorrows and joys, I have not cleansed myself of the war. The horror of those four years is still in me. I bear the mark. All survivors bear the mark." He feels ashamed because he did not have the courage to become a deserter. What disgusts him most with war is its imbecility. If he felt constantly the sensation of fear in his war experience, it was "because it is stupid, because it is useless"; he can understand, however, the value of sacrifice in a just cause, for he has cared for those with contagious and mortal maladies without thought of protecting himself. Here for the first time we see Giono's identification of war with the capitalistic system: "The capitalist state considers human life as the true raw material for the production of capital. To produce capital, it needs, at certain moments, war, just as a cabinet maker has need of a plane. We cannot kill war without killing the capitalist state." And Giono concludes his article with a refusal to sacrifice himself except for his own happiness and that of others.

In 1938 he published two short volumes: *Précisions,* in which he seems to qualify his earlier attack on capitalism when he states that the liberation of the proletariat will come from the impossibility of wars rather than the end of wars from the liberation of the proletariat; and *Lettre aux paysans,* in which he bids the peasants become conscientious objectors in order to starve out Parliaments and General Staffs. In *Le Poids du ciel* of the same year he holds World War I responsible for destroying the moral and physical strength of the following generation; the result was the rise of fascism, nazism and communism which could only lead directly to another world war. The only hope which Giono sees for his generation is on the farms: "One civilization, that of the peasants, has saved its men. The peasant soldiers immediately became peasants again."

At the time of Munich, September 11, 1938, Giono signed with Alain and Victor Marguerite a telegram to Daladier and Chamberlain asking them to save the peace. To his great disappointment, André Gide and Roger Martin du Gard refused to sign, although both congratulated him on his courage. In July, 1939, he launched his last appeal against war in his Preface to the book of his friend Lucien Jacques, *Carnets de moleskine.* Shortly after the outbreak of the war in September, Giono was arrested for his pacifistic activities—which, according to Chonez, included the tearing down of mobilization posters—and was imprisoned in the gloomy old Fort Saint-Nicolas in Marseilles.

III *First Imprisonment*

In September 1943 Maurice Wullens, in the pro-Nazi magazine *Jeune Force de France*, bitterly accused Giono of having abjured his pacifist principles by supinely responding to the mobilization summons and by joining the army at Digne on the sixth day of mobilization, though Giono had declared categorically in *Refus d'obeissance* and in *Précisions* that he would never obey such an order. The spiteful animus of Wullen's excoriation is clearly evident in his contemptuous phrases: "Without a word. Like the least of the wretched anonymous cowards subject to call. He shut his big mouth as soon as the white posters and gendarmes in blue brought him back to reality."

Wullens is technically correct, and yet the bare statement of this Vichyite does a grave injustice to the integrity of Giono. The true facts concerning this episode, as related by Pugnet, who is far from being a blind worshipper of Giono, seem to have been as follows. When the order for mobilization was given, Giono remained at home until the gendarmes came to seize him and take him to Digne. He had not thought it worth while to flee the gendarmes who were friends and neighbors of his and who would thereby have been put to trouble and embarrassment. The colonel in charge of the recruiting depot was none too anxious to accept this man who seemed quiet enough but was full of "subversive" ideas. "Let him stay at the hotel," he said, "and do anything he wants so long as he doesn't set foot in the barracks." Then the Propaganda Service asked Giono to write pacifist tracts for distribution over Germany, a request Giono refused because it would not promise to drop these over all of Europe. An invitation to dinner by the Prefect of the Basses Alpes had no effect on Giono's obstinacy, and the Ministry in a fit of anger sent him to prison in Marseilles.

In his autobiographical *Noé*, Giono has given many interesting details on his incarceration: "High on the horizon and closing entirely the end of Canebière street, rises in the form of a crown the magnificent construction of the fort Saint-Nicolas. The great wall of the fort facing me is terminated on the left by a beautiful promontory like the prow of a ship. It is exactly in this prow that I had my cell." On his arrival at the fort, his head was shaved and he was clad in a smock bearing the number 2,154. The first twenty days were spent in solitary confinement without any light, and his only provisions were a jug of water and half a loaf of bread every four days. Far from being embittered by this treatment, Giono recalls having said to his jailor on being removed from solitary: "For the confinement to be unbearable, you ought to feed the prisoner pheasants and lobsters. Then he would react frantically against his walls. But with my half loaf of bread and jug of water every four days, what did they expect me to do but dream. And they were quite without power to confine my dreams."

When he was at last removed from his solitary cell, he was allowed to go into the courtyard chained to a Negro and to an old offender by his ankles and wrists. At first he felt slightly embarrassed at the admiration shown him by his comrades—who included professional thieves and a murderer—because he had been able to endure twenty days of solitary without "going off his rocker" or even losing his good humor. Obviously, he must be a tough one; and they rejoiced because he had been able to turn the tables on his oppressors. Giono was careful not to undeceive them, but what he had done was quite incidental and without malice aforethought.

Villeneuve has related several amusing incidents concerning Giono's cellmates, anecdotes which obviously must have come from the novelist's own lips. One of his neighbors in prison was an Alsatian named Muller, a former member of the Foreign Legion and a good patriot, though through some mistake held as a spy. He had secured permission to sweep out the cells of those condemned to forced labor in order to gather grains of tobacco with which he was able to make an average of five cigarettes a day. These cigarettes he then exchanged for a liter of wine which he sold in turn for eighty francs. ("Papa" Muller must have possessed unusual business sagacity, for we learn further in Noé that he had amassed a small fortune selling safety pins to the Indians of the Amazon, pins from which they made necklaces.) Another comrade, also an ex-Legionnaire, after drinking beer one day in the prison canteen, bit the glass and proceeded to eat it down to the stem, which he threw away with the words, "I'm not hungry anymore." Whereupon another prisoner picked up the hard stem which he then crushed in his teeth and swallowed, saying "This will do for me." A final anecdote concerned still another companion named Drouland, a waiter in a restaurant who had been arrested for impersonating an admiral in Toulon. When he saw the red ribbon of the Legion of Honor in Giono's button hole, he is said to have reprimanded him gently: "Don't amuse yourself as I did in wearing decorations. They'll lock you up." It would seem a pity to cast doubt on the authenticity of this titillating story, but Lucien Jacques told me that the authorities had removed Giono's insignia before he entered prison since members of the Legion of Honor cannot be imprisoned.

On emerging from solitary, Giono realized that what he had suffered most was the lack of reading material, but he had told himself more stories than the thousand and one Arabian nights. Apparently this need must have been common to all the prisoners for scarcely had Giono been locked up in his new cell when he heard his name called in a low voice by someone asking him if he wanted a book. His benefactor, pressed against the bars of his cell like a monkey, tried to push a volume of Alexandre Dumas across the corridor, but Giono's hand could not reach it. Luckily Papa Muller, contrary to regulations, possessed a ruler, used for pushing objects from cell to cell, which made it possible for Giono to secure the book. Naturally, there was no thought of reading in the reddish obscurity; but Giono was satisfied: "The weight, the form of the book gave my hands a magnificent pleasure, quite sufficient for the moment." When next morning in the courtyard Giono opened the book, he was intoxicated with happiness. Though many pages had been torn out, as he held the volume in his hand, Giono felt greater pleasure than he had ever received from any other book, except perhaps *Don Quixote:* "It was not my mind that was famished for a book; it was my eye which was famished for typography."

It was only after leaving prison that Giono learned with amazement that his warden, top sergeant Césari, had been watching him for three weeks with suspicion through a dormer window looking out on the courtyard. Apparently he had heard a rumor that Giono was fomenting a revolt, whereas in truth the novelist was merely telling stories to his comrades seated around him: "Very simple stories, M. Césari; nothing to trouble your sleep; about Tristan and Isolde, Orlando Furioso and Persilé and Sigismonde." (The reader is reminded here of Giono's popularity as a story-teller in his regiment.)

When André Gide heard of Giono's imprisonment, he promptly

telegraphed Lucien Jacques to do everything possible to free him. More than this, he came himself when Giono was taken from prison to be interrogated, making it a point to salute him as a symbolic gesture. In the meantime, Giono's arrest had aroused a storm of protest throughout the world, in Paris and among the students of Yale University. After the intervention of André Gide and the Queen Mother of Belgium a trial court found no grounds to hold him; at the end of November, he was released from prison with a certificate of demobilization.

CHAPTER 12

Giono and Melville

I *Translation of* Moby Dick

WHEN Giono was later asked why he did not write about his stay in prison, he always answered: "My prison book is *Pour saluer Melville.*" While he did not actually begin the composition of this book until after he had regained his freedom, the main outline of the story and much of the atmosphere in which it is bathed resulted directly from his prison experience.

Like most literary Frenchmen, Giono is widely versed in American literature. His favorite among contemporary writers is Faulkner, but for two earlier masters born in the first quarter of the nineteenth century, Walt Whitman and Herman Melville, he has a natural affinity and a deep affection. Since Giono once wrote: "I detest the sea, the mountain is my mother," it may seem puzzling to explain his attraction for the American Conrad, most of whose books have to do with the sea. A letter from Giono to me disposes of this apparent paradox: "Because Melville's sea has the same grandeur as the mountain. I detest only the Mediterranean, I love the ocean."

In November, 1936, Giono, with the collaboration of Lucien Jacques and Joan Smith, began a translation of Melville's *Moby Dick*. The difficulty of the translation, a labor of love which lasted three years, can be guessed from Giono's discussion of Melville's style which concludes his Foreword to *Pour saluer Melville:* "His sentence is at the same time a torrent, a mountain, a sea, I should say a whale if he had not so clearly shown that it is perfectly possible to know the structure of the whale. But like the mountain, the torrent, or the sea the phrase rolls, rises and falls back with all its mystery. It carries away and drowns one. . . . Always it offers a beauty which escapes analysis but is violently striking." If we may judge by the enthusiasm with which the public received the translation, their efforts were successful for, **even** though published in war time (December, 1939), their *Moby Dick* brought in royalties approaching a million francs.

The inception of Giono's interest in translating *Moby Dick* involves two contradictory explanations, one romantic and idealistic by Giono; the other more prosaic and realistic, by his friend Lucien Jacques. A comparison of these two versions is not only amusing but also perhaps of some value in pointing up one of Giono's characteristic traits: his tendency to transform humble facts through the glamour of his poetic imagination. Were we to believe Giono's Foreword to *Pour saluer Melville*, for five or six years at least *Moby Dick* had been his constant companion:

I would carry it with me regularly on my excursions through the hills. Thus at the very moment when I would approach those great solitudes undulating like the sea but motionless, I needed only to sit down, my back against the trunk of a pine tree, pull out of my pocket this book already rippling, in order to feel swelling under me the multiple life of the seas. How many times have I not heard the rigging whistle above my head, the earth moving under my feet like the deck of a whaler, the pine trunk moan and sway against my back like a mast heavy with swollen sails. Raising my eyes from the page, it often seemed to me that Moby Dick was blowing over there beyond the foam of the olive trees in the ebullition of the great oaks. When evening left me alone, I understood better the soul of this purple hero who dominates the whole book; I had to take only a few steps to rejoin him and, as soon as night had fallen, to become him.

It was not difficult then for Giono to make his friend Lucien Jacques share his passion for the book. As they smoked their pipes around the fireside, Giono translated certain passages with enthusiasm; and they decided to make the book available for others.

The actual circumstances, as related by Lucien Jacques to me, are somewhat less colorful. After Jacques had been wounded in World War I, he was sent to a military center in Brittany which included many of the first American volunteers, some of them from Harvard University. During their discussion of American literature, Jacques was told that the best American literature of the sea was by Dana and Melville and that the latter's *Moby Dick* was particularly outstanding. Many years later, when Jacques was visiting Giono, he happened to remark that he had been reading the most astonishing American book about the sea. *"Moby Dick?"*

asked Giono. "What, you are acquainted with it?" "Yes, and no," Giono answered; then he suggested that all three of them (including an English girl, Joan Smith) must translate it and make it better known in France. It was decided that each would make his own word-for-word translation and then they would compare notes. After working hard on his assignment, Jacques wrote Giono several times but always received evasive answers. When he finally went to see Giono, he was exasperated to learn that the latter had not even begun his work, pleading the urgency of other matters. Jacques then read aloud his translation while Giono read the English and next they polished the translation together. With a smile of gentle resignation, Jacques admitted that Giono's imaginative version was of course untrue; but this really did not matter.

II *Origin of* Pour saluer Melville

Even before his imprisonment Giono had planned to have the translation of *Moby Dick* preceded by a brief salutation to Melville, for which the framework was prepared during his hours of solitary confinement in Fort Saint-Nicolas. He had not been able to procure from America the material for a solid study, and he had only a rather sketchy biography of Melville in his possession: "But I had lovingly translated the book and I had the impression, which I still have, of being well acquainted with his heart. His old dead heart. I therefore composed my book on him solely with my prison memories."

The atmosphere in which Giono composed *Pour saluer Melville* in the autumn of 1939 was romantic in the extreme. Since masons were constructing a fireplace in his upstairs study, he had installed himself in the library on the ground floor which was so cold that it was of little use for Giono to light a fire in the big hearth and draw his table ever closer. The darkness of the library, because of the encircling cypress trees, together with the cold and the beating of the wind on the walls, made Giono feel as if he were still behind the bars of Fort Saint-Nicolas.

As he began to write he thought he heard the sound of a skirt, of creaking boots, and of a little cough; and he felt himself grazed by the silhouette of a woman, going towards the bookshelves and melting away in the gilt of the bindings and the bronze of the sheepskins. (The fact that he had not seen her face explains why

Melville in the story at first sees only her hand, then her figure.)
As he was starting to write again, Giono felt himself grazed anew,
heard the same rustling sound and little cough, and smelled a delightful odor of violets and vanilla. If she appeared to him then
with tartan skirt, green stockings, red shoes, woolen jacket of
green and red plaid, and a felt hat with an immense falcon plume
tinted red, the colors represent his hallucinating memories of Fort
Saint-Nicolas; green, from the damp walls covered with moss and
from the faces kept abnormally in darkness and ghastly from the
nourishment of prison fare; red, from the lanterns which made red
reflections on the cells as the guards passed on their rounds and
from the eyelids lowered over eyes which imitated sleep. "It is
thus that Adelina White was born. In truth one cannot say some
one is born when she arrives dressed in red and green plaid with a
falcon-plumed felt hat; I ought to say that this is how I made the
acquaintance of Adelina White, daughter of Saint-Nicolas and of
her works."

III *Résumé*

After a brief discussion of Melville's early life, Giono begins his
story with the visit of Melville to London to discuss with his edi-
tors the publication of his latest book, *White Jacket*. Learning
with surprise that little time is needed to conclude these negoti-
ations, he wonders how he will manage to pass the fortnight before his return sailing. Informed by a stable boy that there is a
charming spot above Bristol called Woodcut, Melville suddenly
decides to take the stagecoach for this destination, after having
acquired from a second hand dealer the complete outfit of a sailor
to replace his conventional attire.

The only other passenger in the coach turns out to be a mysterious lady, whose hand only can he see at first since he is on the box
and she is within the coach; but his romantic reveries are stirred
when the coach is accosted on the lonely Dartmoor plain by two
strangers in peasant attire with whom the mysterious lady con-
verses. When the coach stops for the first night, Melville is too shy
to address his traveling companion, but on the following day he
begins to make her acquaintance. Admitting that he is the American novelist Melville, he learns that her name is Adelina White
and that she is on a mission to smuggle food into starving Ireland.
Soon he hears the story of her life and of her devotion to the

rebels whose outbreaks against the tyranny of England have been
so rigorously repressed. As they ride through the autumn countryside, he makes her feel poetically his own vision of the hillsides
and of the clouds and rain; and, in turn, he falls under the spell of
her idealistic personality.

Back in America he feels equal to the great work swelling
within him, and her frequent letters of encouragement seem to
call forth deeper genius than he has shown in his earlier books. At
last, when *Moby Dick* is finished and receives the plaudits of his
friend Hawthorne and of the entire literary world, Melville remains disconsolate; for the last letter he had received from Adelina White had spoken of a serious illness. When no more letters
come, he is compelled to believe that she has died; but the question which torments him is whether she had been able to read his
masterpiece before death came. Without her inspiration, his next
two books, *Pierre* and *Israel Potter,* are only drudgery; and, recognizing their mediocrity, he solicits a position as customs inspector
in 1857. When he died after thirty-four years of total silence, his
last words to his nurse were to ask if a letter had come from England.

IV *Affinity with Melville*

As testimony to the apparent veracity of this narrative, it is interesting to note that even the granddaughter of the American
novelist did not doubt its authenticity. An explanation of the impression of actual reality which the book makes on the reader may
be found in the naturalness with which this incident is inserted
between factual accounts of Melville's youth and old age; the
vivid atmosphere of English inns and rolling countryside which
have quite a Dickensian flavor; and finally—as if to relieve the
mind of any doubting Thomas—the closing paragraph of thanks
to a Mrs. Una Stephen Barrow for "the unpublished documents
which permitted me to salute Melville." Of course, the story is
really only another example of Giono's capacity for flying off on
the wings of his poetic imagination, and he has confirmed to me
that the entire episode was invented without any factual basis
whatever.

As Pugnet has shrewdly observed, whenever Giono has written
of other authors, he has done the work not of a critic but of a
romantic creator: "At each page one feels that the two writers

belong to the same spiritual family; the author of *Moby Dick* was a big robust fellow . . . free from any prejudice, like Giono himself. Giono sees in Melville a friend. And he immediately makes him one of his characters."

The most subjective part of the book, in which the identification of Melville and Giono is complete, is the long soliloquy in which Melville expresses his philosophy as an author. Prophetic of Giono's own preoccupation with extending the scope of his subject matter and style are these words: "No, he certainly doesn't want to continue to write the little books he knows how to make. Work has no interest unless it is a perpetual combat with the broad unknown." Typical of Giono's dissatisfaction concerning his critics is the following: "With the book he has just written . . . he is going to be taken for a rebel. People like classification. He is a rebel only because he is a poet . . . 'I express myself; I am incapable of expressing any other than myself . . . I create what I am and that is what a poet is' . . . Not a man of letters for one penny." However accurate may be this characterization of Melville's rugged non-conformity and independence, it is at least equally typical of Giono's own personality.

V *Turning Point*

How much influence did Giono's affinity with Melville have upon his own work, since Giono claims to have read with delight everything Melville ever wrote? To this query, he replied with a vigorous negative, giving two reasons: the late date in his own life when he first came to know Melville, and the impossibility of carrying over into French anything of Melville's very individual style. Without questioning Giono's sincerity, it is nevertheless possible to observe here the beginning of a new tone and emphasis in his work. The heroine, Adelina White, elegant, delicate, passionate and somewhat mysterious, represents a type we have not found previously among the gallery of Giono's feminine portraits. Credit again must be given to Pugnet for being the first to point out that, starting with *Pour saluer Melville*, Giono begins to give us, instead of realistic peasant characters taken from everyday life, "personages somewhat romantic, refined, elegant, and often of astounding lucidity." Many of the feminine characters in Giono's post-war *Chroniques* have traits in common with Adelina White. In connection with this new heroine, Pugnet emphasizes also the ascending order of spiritualization of love in Giono's work, from carnal love in *Naissance de l'Odyssée,* through natural instinct and necessity, then adoration for a virgin, then renouncement of love out of respect for another. "Finally announcing the *Chroniques, Pour saluer Melville* contains a painting of love very delicate, very softly shaded, the truest perhaps that Giono has achieved. . . . This leads to those exceptional passions of the later books; the strongest of these sentiments is that exclusive attachment, that unreflecting and absolute love felt by the Numance couple (*Les Ames fortes*) or Angélo and Pauline (*le Hussard*)."

Although Giono's tribute to Melville, like his translation of *Moby Dick,* was well received by the French public, it has perhaps not obtained from most critics the attention it deserves. From this discussion, it should be evident that Herman Melville and his work struck a responsive chord in his French translator and biographer. In the strict sense of the word it may be less a case of American influence on Giono than of remarkable, not to say miraculous, affinity. At any rate, one must render homage to the highly poetic quality of the narrative of *Pour saluer Melville,* the romantic atmosphere of the setting, and the delicate shading of this ideal love. Even if this brief tale did not attract us through its own excellence it would be significant, as already suggested, for marking the turning point between Giono's early rustic realism and his later more sophisticated, romantic, and mysterious *Chroniques.* If *Pour saluer Melville* does not throw further light on the great American master of the sea, it offers an illuminating insight into Giono's own philosophy of life as well as his technique of composition. Giono is such a complicated literary phenomenon that it would be idle to seek one work which characterizes him completely. In no other volume, however, do we glimpse the true Giono more vividly than in this delightful *Pour saluer Melville.*

CHAPTER 13

Second Imprisonment and
Literary Quarantine

I *Prison Again*

DURING the war years Giono published four important books: *Pour saluer Melville* (1941), *Triomphe de la vie* (1942), *Le Bout de la route* and other plays (1943), and *L'Eau vive*, a collection of essays and short stories (1944). The last two volumes, however, were composed many years before; and, for the greater part, they had already appeared in magazines. Except for a trip to Paris in 1942 in connection with the staging of his plays, Giono remained quietly at home, working steadily on his later *Chroniques*. If we may judge from an interview published early in 1943,[1] Giono showed an almost incredible capacity for continuing the daily routine of his life, as if the war did not even exist. He rose at four in the morning, made his coffee, smoked his first pipe, and then, except for intermissions to fill his pipe, wrote steadily until noon. After lunch he took long walks in the afternoon regardless of the state of the weather; then, after looking over the last pages written in the morning, he went early to bed. The only break in this regular routine occurred one day a week when Giono hopped on his bicycle and rode to one or the other of his two farms some forty kilometers distant to discuss with his overseers the purchase or sale of horses and sheep, or the acquisition of necessary tools or machines.

After the liberation of southern France, the Communists began a reign of terror in the region surrounding Manosque and Aix. Shocking and sometimes mistaken vengeance was wreaked by former Resistance fighters on all suspected of collaboration with the Nazis—Giono himself saw a woman shot during the reprisals. Giono was suspect on two accounts; he had never spoken out against the Occupation or the measures taken by Vichy to appease the Nazis, and he had published an interview in the first number of *La Gerbe*, July 11, 1940, the reactionary journal of collaborator

Alphonse de Chateaubriant. In Giono's *Triomphe de la vie* the glorification of rustic life and the joys of the artisan seemed in accord with the social philosophy of Marshal Pétain. It was claimed by Giono's accusers that his books were translated in Nazi Germany and that his publication was protected by the official Agency of the Press in Paris under German domination. Giono was arrested and confined for six months in the prison at Digne.

Villeneuve, usually quite accurate where the biography of Giono is concerned, seems in error when he states that Giono's innocence "did not prevent a regional prefect, who was French only in name, from having him imprisoned in Saint-Vincent-les-Forts." Giono, on the other hand, stated categorically to me that he was sent to prison by one of his best friends—not to punish him but to save his life from extreme danger. This version was corroborated by Lucien Jacques, who added that, when Madame Giono tried to free her husband, she was dissuaded by the friend who had imprisoned him, with the argument that Giono was much safer where he was.

For his earlier incarceration in Fort Saint-Nicolas at the outbreak of war, Giono feels not the slightest resentment, finding it quite natural and logical that the authorities took this attitude towards his pacifist activities. When he talks of the retaliation of Communists at the war's close, however, his eyes flash with an anger unusual to him. Yet his actual imprisonment at Digne seems to have had its agreeable, even amusing, side. He was given permission to cut wood for exercise and to receive packages from home. During the serious illness of his mother, he was even allowed to return under the surveillance of guards who apparently enjoyed this experience so much that, when his mother was better and it was time to return to jail, it was Giono himself, he remarked with a smile, who had to escort his guards back to prison. When the Communists were ousted from the region a few weeks later, Giono was promptly freed without ever coming to trial.

II *The Evidence*

Without attempting to whitewash Giono or to claim that there was anything particularly heroic in his passivity towards the conquerors of his country, there is nevertheless much to be said in his defense. First, Pugnet, while reproaching Giono for having published texts during the Occupation without considering whether these might be of service to the enemy, nevertheless refuses to blame him for having remained apart from the conflict since Giono felt that the values he cherished were not at stake. Second, in regard to the article in *La Gerbe* and to *Triomphe de la vie,* these did nothing more than express themes already dear to Giono long before the war. It would be preposterous to think for a moment that "this singer of liberty, this enemy of the military and the police state, this destroyer of official values could have had any sympathy for the government of the Marshal." As will be seen in the following chapter, the play which Giono wrote during the war, *Voyage en calèche,* is decidedly anti-Nazi in tone.

Third, while it is true that Giono was allowed publication under Nazi authorities and was eulogized in some pro-Nazi magazines such as *Signal,* a study of the collaborationist press shows that with few exceptions the writers were contemptuous if not openly hostile towards Giono. A bitter article in the January 29, 1943, issue of *Suis Partout* pours ridicule on the interview quoted above from *Paris Midi;* it calls the author's morning program "Ego Giono" and his buying and selling of animals "Posterity take notice." The reader will recall Wullen's spiteful attitude towards Giono's acceptance of mobilization, which he claimed was motivated by Giono's hatred of Hitler. In *Jeune Force de France* for January, 1943, Philippe Merlin, one of Giono's youthful disciples of the Contadour, sheds crocodile tears in bidding farewell to his former idol who he thinks has prostituted his poetic gifts for material gain. An anonymous writer in *Révolution Nationale* for February 2 of the same year, commenting favorably on the apostasy of Philippe Merlin, overflows with venom concerning Giono: "The hill, the man, the land, the grain were decoys. . . . The pastor was a charlatan, the high priest a sharper; the shepherd, a quack." Finally a scribbler in the same review for August 24, 1943, calling Giono "the Tolstoi of the evening school," likens his writing to a sort of *ratatouille* (stew) *niçoise;* and he ridicules Giono's effrontery to speak "on a footing of equality with the stars, with the elements, with the trees—and with men—in the manner of a prophet who has heard the Bible discussed in public school by a teacher belonging to the League for the Rights of Man." Although this hostility of Nazi sycophants may be considered not germane to Giono's defense, it proves at any rate that Giono inspired no more sympathy among Fascists than among Communists. For a recluse as solitary as Giono, it was something of a triumph to have infuriated at the same time both extremes of the political spectrum.

In regard to Giono's personal conduct during the Occupation, no one has produced a shred of evidence that he was ever a collaborator—not that he was not often approached on the subject. To my direct and perhaps tactless questioning, Giono replied that Hitler and his emissaries had indeed tried to involve him in their cause. Because of fear of reprisals against his wife and daughters, Giono, instead of giving flat refusals, managed to find an excuse, such as illness, to decline such offers until at last the Nazis gave him up in disgust. It is possible that the campaign of vilification against Giono in the French Fascist press, too sustained as we have seen to be purely spontaneous, may have been actuated by this Nazi disappointment. It remains true of course that Giono never joined the Resistance because of his very human, if unheroic, fear of retaliation against his family. On the other hand we have the authority of his biographer Villeneuve for stating that Giono did advise young labor draftees not to leave for Germany and that he put one of his farms at their disposal. He also rendered many services to Jews, including the composer Meyerowitz; he did such things as keep their dangerous papers and packages in his house.

III *Blacklist*

More painful to Giono than his incarceration at Digne must have been the action of the Comité National des Ecrivains, in their decision published September 9, 1944, to blacklist his future publications. Since this list included all writers suspected in any degree of collaboration with the Nazis—not only Giono but Jouhandeau, Céline, Montherlant, Paul Morand and many other famous names—it would be advisable to sketch briefly this entire episode which looms so large in the development of contemporary French literature. Once more I must express my obligation to Professor B. R. Jordan of Duke University for his helpful information concerning the conflict between Resistance and collaborationist writers at the war's close.

Early in the war the Comité National des Ecrivains was

founded as a writer's section of the Comité National de Libération Française. It was established by Jacques Decour, writer, lycée professor, and pre-war director of the Communist review *Commune* (who later was killed by the Germans); but the founding committee also included Jean Paulhan, Jacques Debû-Bridel, Charles Vildrac, Jean Guéhenno, and Jean Blanzet. The purpose of the Comité was to embrace all literary Résistants, support the ideals of the Resistance, and legislate on all matters relating to the status of writers. In 1942 the group began the clandestine publication of *Les Lettres Françaises,* founded by Jacques Decour and Jean Paulhan. By the end of the war the Comité seems to have reached its greatest prestige, numbering then among its membership most of the leading figures in French literature: Duhamel, Valéry and Mauriac from the Académie Française; Claudel, Gide* and Schlumberger from the *Nouvelle Revue Française;* the Nobel prize-winner Roger Martin du Gard; and Sartre, Camus,* André Rousseaux, Malraux, and others.

With the liberation of France, the various Resistance groups which had merged into the Forces Françaises de l'Intérieur felt their first duty was to punish collaborators. In September, 1944, the Comité National des Ecrivains therefore drew up an extensive blacklist of writers suspected of anything milder than the resistance concept of patriotism, and it also pledged to contribute nothing to any periodical or publishing house which accepted the works of a collaborator. As Professor Jordan says, "in most cases the offenders had committed no crime specifically covered by law and the *CNE* wished to enforce a moral (and perhaps economic) penalty."

Soon, however, the feverish pitch of this threatened witch-hunt began to cool off when some of the most respected writers in the Resistance uttered pleas for tolerance and moderation. As early as October, 1944, Mauriac protested against the intolerance, self-righteousness, and exclusiveness of the Committee, contending that the principle of personal liberty was sufficiently vital in France to permit the right of expression even to the followers of Pétain and Maurras. Camus,[2] feeling that the interests of reconstruction demanded "neither victims nor executioners," expressed

* Both Gide and Camus were to become winners of the Nobel prize for literature.

his indignation in an article published in December of the same year: "I hear attacks on every hand against the *Résistance* and the *Résistants*. They have much to account for. They attribute to themselves the merit for a liberation due only to the Allies, . . . they live on hatred and injustice." Camus insisted that suffering and meritorious service during the war conferred no special rights. Paulhan claimed for a writer the "right to make a mistake"; and, in a highly controversial article, he compared the position of the so-called collaborators to that of Romain Rolland in World War I. In an open letter to the members of the *CNE* Paulhan accused the members not only of cruelty but of hypocrisy, pointing out startling anti-national quotations from earlier utterances by Benda, Romain Rolland, Eluard and Aragon.[3] Soon it became apparent that the *CNE* was being steered too closely to the Communist party line, and the resignations began to pour in—first Mauriac, Camus and Jean Paulhan—until it had lost most of its more distinguished adherents and become chiefly an organ of the extreme left.

In 1948 André Gide generously came to the defense of Giono and the others who had been "purged" by discussing the pages of his *Journal* which betrayed his own first depression at the invasion of France in 1940: "I had the right to hope that those pages would temper the fury of the accusations made against the Gionos, Jouhandeaux, the Montherlants, against those who were deceived. That mistake of judgment was mine, too. I could be reproached as they were; I gave proof of it. If you condemn them, condemn me in the same way."[4] Since legal prosecution was out of the question, the quarantine was ineffective; and Giono and the other alleged collaborators were soon free to publish as before. One of them, indeed, Montherlant, has recently been elected to the French Academy, the first to receive this honor without going through the traditional rites of candidacy and personal calls on the members for their support.

As an epilogue to this reversal of public opinion, it may not be without interest to contrast the bitterness shown Giono at the time and the amazing rejuvenation of his reputation and popularity that soon took place. In October, 1944, Tristan Tzara was scurrilously calling Giono "a novelist of cowardice" whose characters are all weaklings in the face of nature and who collaborated with Germans in Paris while being anti-Hitler in the South: "Every where the Boche manifested himself . . . this clever merchant of words, merchant of human lives, merchant in short, showed himself in the nudity of his ignominy." [5] It is a far cry from this nadir to which Giono's reputation had fallen to the dazzling success of his post-war writings.

CHAPTER 14

Return to the Theater

I Le Voyage en calèche (1947)

IN the interview for the magazine *Carrefour*,[1] Giono made the candid confession in regard to his dramatic production: "I must finish up my play in three days, otherwise, beginning with the second act, the novelist will get the upper hand and it won't be theater any more. That is what happened to me with *Le Voyage en calèche*. The first act was good, and the other two frankly were bad." This statement is an example of the remarkable lucidity and objectivity which Giono shows towards his own work; moreover, it proves his realization that his own genius was primarily that of the novelist rather than the dramatist. For this reason, perhaps, he has not called *Le Voyage en calèche* a play or a drama but "un divertissement romantique en trois actes."

Written in 1942 during the Occupation, the play was first presented in Paris in June, 1944, just before the Allied landings in Normandy which soon resulted in the closing of the theater. This play, laid in Piedmont after the invasion of the French armies in 1797, reminds one of a melodrama of Hugo—in particular of *Hernani*—because of its picturesque setting, its poetic imagery, and its mysterious hero Julio, who, like Hernani, is a disguised nobleman turned bandit with a price upon his head. Yet Giono's hero differs radically from the Hernani who felt himself a blind force urged on by fate, for Julio exults in his own independence and intellectual subtlety in foiling the projects of the French invaders of Italy.

As Giono stated, the first act is excellent in its dramatic suspense, though perhaps too long (one hundred twenty-five pages) and at times too overloaded with clever banter. The bandit Consalvo (Julio), disguised as a valet in the country home of the famous Milanese opera singer Fulvia, is the object of pursuit by Colonel Vincent and his French troops. As the Colonel sets out to scour the countryside, Julio, now dressed as an impeccable aristocrat, forces Fulvia to drive off with him in her barouche. They find refuge in a feudal castle whose owner, no lover of General

Napoleon, agrees to protect them. When the Colonel appears at the door, he is received by Julio in the guise of proprietor of the château and is offered hot punch by the latter's servant John. Suspecting, however, that Julio is really the bandit Consalvo, the Colonel demands to see the mistress of the castle; and, while he stands dumfounded at being confronted with Fulvia to whom he had been making amorous declarations only a few hours before, Julio makes his escape. Torn between love and his sense of duty, the Colonel conducts Fulvia to prison in Milan.

In the second act Fulvia is in her loge at La Scala, having been released from prison long enough to give an operatic performance for the benefit of the French officers. Acclaimed frenetically for her singing, she snubs the invaders by contemptuously refusing to accept a curtain call. The Colonel enters her loge to inform her that the French plan to execute her at dawn, and he hopes that Consalvo will fall into the trap of trying to rescue her. At this moment they are joined by Julio, who has had his valet John counterfeit twenty signatures of Napoleon to dispatch his troops in various directions and to issue a pardon for Fulvia. Fulvia now realizes that it is the chivalrous bandit, not the French Colonel, whom she really loves though Julio informs her (falsely) that he is not a nobleman but the illegitimate offspring of a priest and a woman of the people; then he closes the door upon Fulvia and the Colonel.

In the final act Fulvia and the Colonel are seated on a knoll overlooking the plain swarming with French troops who are on the march before dawn to attack Austria. Fulvia has agreed to marry the Colonel and to follow him to glamorous adventure as he forces open the capitals of Europe. When the Colonel leaves her for a few moments to make arrangements for her carriage, Julio suddenly arrives to express his disdain of the course she has chosen. Soon after he leaves and the Colonel reappears, John informs them that Julio, who was indeed of noble birth, has just been killed by the saber of a French captain.

Thinking he must have courted death deliberately as a result of her coldness, Fulvia now refuses to depart with the Colonel, who seems to her petty and vulgar in contrast with the mysterious and poetic dreamer, Julio. When Julio reappears very much alive, she is furious at first with his deception, but she soon realizes it is he whom she truly loves. Though John offers to find them a country *berline* with thick oak walls which would be proof against the bullets of the soldiers, both the lovers refuse; they choose instead a *barouche* as "ostentatious as a fruit cup." A few moments later we hear the shots fired by the platoon which intercepted them.

The parallel between the situation in this play and the Nazi occupation of France is so obvious that one wonders how Giono was able to have it performed. It is true that he employed certain camouflage which may have blinded Hitler's agents to its real message: Napoleon is obviously not Hitler, and Giono even stresses the fact that he is really an Italian who would be amused rather than angry at the clever forgeries of his name. Julio asserts likewise that, if he is the adversary of an army, it is not through patriotism: "I place my country too high to imagine that it can be soiled in any way by the passage or the sojourn of a few French troopers." But for any Frenchman at the time the analogy must have been transparent enough when Giono expresses the amazement of the Colonel who finds the peasant looking through him as if he did not exist: "I didn't bother him any more than a pane of glass." The baseness of French "quislings" is of course suggested by the willingness of Prima to act as a front for the occupying forces. And, when the Colonel boasts, "from all the ramparts of your mountain villages it is our cannons which command the valleys," Fulvia has only to remind him gently, "Colonel, il y a l'esprit" to express the powerlessness of the military might over the inner consciences of the people. Finally, Julio expresses the relief he felt when he came to understand the petty materialism of the invaders beneath their hollow façade of military glory: "When I saw you pass between the branches of the beech tree with your lean faces, your eyes fixed, biting your lips, I feared the competition of a great idea. Now I see you spading up peacefully a little plot of ground with good bourgeois arms, sleeves rolled up. I had dreaded a kind of new Grail." Could this statement not express Giono's scorn for the principles of National Socialism which declared it would establish a new order to last a thousand years and which was only motivated by lust and greed?

Le Voyage en calèche with its two hundred fifty pages, its mingling of poetic lyricism, fusillade of wit, ideational symbolism, and metaphysical abstraction would certainly have been more successful as a novel than as a drama. Yet, if the heroes of this drama seem abstract types and closer to those of the Middle Ages than to either the classical or the contemporary stage, the ideas which they represent are interesting for the reader, all the more so since they belie so clearly the unfair imputation that Giono ever sympathized with the invader. A revision entitled *La Calèche* was very successful in Paris 1965–66.

II   Joseph à Dothan (Joseph et ses frères)

In the winter of 1952 Giono was requested to make a French adaptation of the seventeenth-century Dutch play *Joseph at Dothan* by Joost van den Vondel for performance before the Queen of the Netherlands in the Roman theater of Orange the following summer. When Giono accepted the task on condition that he might use prose instead of the alexandrine verse of the original, opposition developed in Dutch circles in Paris, particularly on the part of a Dutch poet who claimed to have already translated the play into French verse. Giono thereupon offered to renounce the project but was persuaded to undertake it by the Dutch Embassy which, despite its knowledge of the verse translation, still preferred to have Giono make the adaptation in prose.

Without acquaintance with the original play of Vondel it is of course impossible to determine how much the merit of the French production owes to Giono. Since Giono does not read Dutch, he was furnished a literal word-for-word translation by Monsieur J. Plessens. We have, however, Giono's own statement that he allowed himself no liberties with the text, other than the concluding three-page monologue of Reuben; this was almost entirely his own invention since he felt the original text would have satisfied no one. It must be granted that this addition by Giono forms a fitting ending, for it adds a touch of psychological verity in its portrayal of Reuben's remorse; and its sonorous, rhythmic prose is in keeping with the rest of this moving drama.

Since Jacob's sons obviously did not wear boots, Giono concludes from Vondel's mention of this word that he must have represented his actors in costumes of their own day. He recommended, therefore, the use of 1952 costumes in order to accentuate the universality of this drama of ignominy and jealousy.

III   Domitien

Giono's recent play *Domitien*, commissioned for the Paris radio, proves once more that his true genius is that of a novelist, not a dramatist. The play contains a rather loosely connected series of scenes depicting the last months in the life of the Roman emperor, Domitian, including his campaign against the Dacians. Almost at the opening of the play we have a forewarning of the dissension among the populace and its indignation against the tyrant, and we learn later of the plot between his divorced wife Domitia and his favorite general Vibius to assassinate him. Yet Giono has not sought to create a situation of dramatic suspense; the murderers seem truly reluctant to commit the fatal deed and Domitian himself, in his attitude of satiety and philosophic disdain, appears almost to welcome the tragic dénouement.

In the characters of Vibius and Domitia, Giono has not been successful in giving us clearcut individuals. The former, perhaps still under the spell of close association from childhood with the tyrant he once admired as a "prince de la jeunesse," actually defends him from the revolution brewing in Rome by executing several of the ringleaders. Apparently it is only when Vibius realizes that his own life is in danger from the capricious humor of his master that he decides to slay him; Domitia, likewise, susceptible to her husband's charm in spite of his cruelty and philandering, seems strangely without motivation in her share of the conspiracy.

What relieves the somberness of this tragedy is Giono's skill in presenting the picturesque silhouettes of the dwarf and soothsayer. The dwarf in particular is titillating in his impudent flashes of wit, which remind one of Musset's buffoon, Fantasio. Requested by Domitian to show Vibius the ear which the emperor had cut off in a fit of rage, he replies: "Spare my modesty, Sire, I do not like to display my war wounds." And, when the dwarf decides against seeking safety in flight because he too has a sense of pride, he appeals to our pity and our sense of humor at the same time with his remark: "Don't I have viscera too like those of everybody, although tiny ones."

Yet Giono's chief purpose in writing this play was obviously to paint a portrait of Emperor Domitian, whose subtle, complicated personality challenged the creator of *Un Roi sans divertissement*. Giono has stated that his intention was to emphasize the lonely solitude of the emperor as a tragic figure, but the dominating characteristic of Domitian for most readers (quite in accordance with historical tradition) may appear to be cruelty, pursued to the limit of sadism, as in his decree to have the three erring vestal virgins quartered and the twelve portions distributed in various sections of the city to rot in summer heat. As the dwarf remarks, the man whom Domitian kills at one stroke can consider himself fortunate in comparison with whole families reduced to sausage meat. When Vibius tries to excuse Domitian's brutality on the grounds of illness, Domitia reminds him that the emperor enjoys robust health and lucid intelligence. Domitian takes pleasure in prolonging the anguish of his victims; he toys with his soothsayer, for instance, as a cat plays with a mouse. His only reaction to the stench from the burning bodies of the Dacians is an expression of disgust that their executioners had not waited until his departure, in order to spare him this nausea.

Though Domitia, discussing her husband with Vibius, remarks that one cannot caress a dog with two heads, Domitian is far from being merely a monster. He is also a voluptuary, and few Roman women remain unsusceptible to his charm. He is also highly cultured and can describe the delicate joys of autumn with the poetry of Virgil's *Georgics*. In fact, his sophistication makes him all the more terrifying; and the dwarf finds barbarians sweet to imagine since Domitian has become civilized.

As already suggested, however, Domitian was in Giono's eyes one more in the long line of solitary heroes of whom he had given so many striking portraits in his novels. The final qualities, therefore, which impart a sense of mysterious depth and complexity to his character, are his insatiable curiosity for plumbing what is beyond reality, and his romantic disillusionment and detachment from the pleasures of glory, voluptuousness, and even sadistic cruelty. Though he seems unaccountably fearful of a revolution from the Roman populace, he appears at last so lonely in his isolated grandeur, so sated and bored with existence, that he welcomes the assassin's dagger as one final new sensation for his jaded palate.

CHAPTER 15

Les Chroniques

I A Change of Manner

WHEN the first volume of Giono's *Chroniques, Un Roi sans divertissement*, appeared in 1947, the astonishment of literary critics was evident, for many spoke of Giono's "second manner." Giono does not deny the change in his manner of writing which began with this volume, but he insists that it is not due to the war or to his imprisonment but had its inception much earlier: the first part of *Le Hussard sur le toit* was written at the same period as the last of his epic novels: "I merely say that there is no sudden change, but rather an evolution for which the causes go back much earlier." A close examination of his works indeed indicates that his genius is extremely mobile, always in the process of development and modification, so that it might be more correct to speak of a fourth or fifth manner rather than merely a second one. Thus, after the youthful ebullience and humorous parody of the *Odyssey*, we have seen the compact and sober *Trilogy of Pan*, then the cosmic lyricism of the great nature epics, followed by the period of social reform and pacifist protest against war.

Incarcerated at the outbreak of World War II and again during Communist control after the overthrow of Vichy, Giono's disgrace had seemed complete when he was refused the right to publish one of his books in a de luxe edition. Rarely if ever has there been a more dramatic reversal of fortune than that experienced by Giono with the publication of his *Chroniques*. The outward signs of the new popularity have been the award of the million franc Monaco Prize and election to the Goncourt Academy.

Although the novels of the Hussard series are included under Giono's new rubric *Chroniques*, it seems best to discuss them in a separate chapter and to limit our discussion here to the five books which are independent of the cycle. According to Marcel Arland, Giono calls these volumes *Chroniques* not because they are chronicles of a period of society but because they represent a new method of story telling: "In his new works, recitals, reports, testimonies take on indeed extreme importance." [1] The chief difference between these books and the earlier volumes of Giono is their subordination of lyric description of nature to an objective presentation of character. To quote Arland again: "Formerly his novels tended to create a myth and struck us first of all by their character of lyric epic. His protagonists were so closely bound up with nature that they were somewhat submerged by it. . . . To be sure, nature is always present in Giono's new novels . . . but it occupies less space, it is no longer the chief character, it serves as background and support; men on the other hand do not cease to grow until they are sufficient for the interest of the book."

Among the many critics favorably impressed by Giono's evolution as a novelist was Maurice Nadeau, who has observed: "Effecting a transformation of which there are few examples, he remains of course Jean Giono, but how can one fail to observe that his limitation has enriched him, that he has become more authentic in becoming more skilful and that now he appears natural, almost without affectation." [2] Nadeau points out an interesting paradox: though these stories proceed from the imagination of the author and create for us a world full of strangely romantic mystery, this world nevertheless is "more solid, more human and more logical at the same time, more 'contemporary' perhaps than that modern world in which he used to set his characters." Yet "mysterious and brutal, romantic and harsh, peopled with tragic madmen," it remains a novelist's world.

A second difference between the *Chroniques* and the earlier novels of Giono is their objective detachment; the only intervention of the author is a certain irony *à la Stendhal*, the writer who in recent years has been closest to his heart. As Pugnet has suggested: "It seems that henceforth the production of a book is for Giono a technical problem to solve, a game to play well, a match to win." Whereas many of Giono's early characters, such as Bobi or Saint-Jean, seemed to incarnate subjectively the novelist's own deepest aspirations, Giono now appears to take lightly even his favorite heroes, without however diminishing in any way their tragic quality.

The technique by which Giono achieves this new objectivity in the *Chroniques* is to have the story related in the first person by one or more individuals, usually of humble station and often of mediocre intelligence, whose stupidity or prejudice is evident to the reader. "It is succulent for the writer to have the drama related by a comic personage," Giono has remarked. There are certain drawbacks of course, in this technique of a "tale told by an idiot." Though it forces Giono to subordinate his tendency to verbosity, there remain occasional outbursts of lyric splendor which we would only regretfully forego but which seem incongruous in the mouth of the peasant narrator. Furthermore, the confusion, repetition, and occasional conflicts in testimony sometimes tend to irritate and perplex the reader. On the other hand, this form of narration gives vividness and realism which render the most fantastic adventures credible.

II Un Roi sans divertissement

The opening scene of *Un Roi sans divertissement* (1947) is equaled perhaps only by that of *Colline* for plunging the reader into an atmosphere of dread and of tragic foreboding. For twenty days the snow has been falling without respite on the little mountain village:

At noon everything is covered, everything rubbed out; there is no more world, no more sound, nothing. Some heavy columns of mist flow along the roofs and shroud the houses. One o'clock, two, three, the snow continues to fall. Four o'clock; night; the hearths are lighted; it is snowing. Five o'clock, six, seven; the lamps are lit, it is snowing. Outside there is no longer any earth, nor sky, nor village, nor mountain; there is only the crumbling mass of this thick icy powder of a world which must have burst.

In his interesting discussion of Giono's techniques in expressing the passage of time, Pierre Robert[3] has chosen this example to illustrate the author's search for new procedures.

Some critics have termed *Un Roi sans divertissement* "un roman policier," and it cannot be denied that much of its hold upon the reader, particularly in the first long episode, is that of a crime and detection story. There are, however, merits of a more literary nature. If the haunting atmosphere of the snowfall in the opening chapter serves primarily to deepen the sense of impending tragedy, there is a poetic evocation of the magic wrought by the gold of autumn in the forest and in particular on the majestic beech tree which is not merely an artistic hors d'oeuvre but an essential element in the drama.

However, the greatest interest in the novel lies in the depiction of character. It is true that this interest is concentrated almost entirely on the enigmatic person of the hero, Langlois. His three friends are little more than picturesque silhouettes. Of the *procureur royal* we remember chiefly the enormous stomach which he is always pushing in front of him. Mme Tim, the graceful créole of sixty who looks half her age and is the exotic product of a Mexican convent located between a volcano and a glacier, interests us, as Pugnet has shown, chiefly as an elegant prolongation of the earlier Adelina White. Saucisse, the massive sexagenarian who had risen from her early life as a prostitute to the proprietorship of the village café, seems a rather incongruous mixture with her obscene cursing and her sentimental adoration of Langlois.

Langlois, however, is one of Giono's most fascinating characters. Commander of Wolf Hunting, Langlois makes an impressive figure on his prancing horse. His nickeled gun is perfectly greased, his coat is of the finest wool, his breeches are of velvet, and his boots immaculate. Though courteous, he holds himself aloof from the populace. Like a monk, he seems in contemplation of another world; like a soldier, he is abrupt and accustomed to have his orders obeyed without explanation. Called by one critic a monster, this puzzling man, whose harshness filled the villagers with awed respect, is yet capable of friendship with the devoted Saucisse; with his old comrade-in-arms, the *procureur royal;* and especially with the aristocratic and delicate Mme Tim. Langlois is also sensitive and considerate of others, for we see his respect for the assassin as a human being; his concern, perhaps tinged with remorse, for the widow of the assassin he had shot; and his gallant treatment of Saucisse, not as a retired prostitute but as a lady to whom deference and respect are due.

Much of his attraction for the reader is doubtless due to the unexplained riddle of his character. Why does Langlois commit suicide so soon after an apparently congenial marriage? What is the relationship of Langlois to the murderer whom he so courteously removes from this world rather than turn him over to a court of justice to be hanged, and why does he appear to have a feeling of guilt in regard to the assassin's widow? What is the symbolism involved in Langlois' fascination with the blood of the goose upon the snow shortly before he commits suicide? Does Langlois take his own life because, as Pugnet suggests, he is ashamed of his profession as policeman (a strange theory, since Langlois has been raised to the distinguished rank of *Commandeur de louveterie*)? A more logical deduction inherent in the author's quotation at the end from Pascal, "un roi sans divertissement est un homme plein de misères"—seems to be that Langlois, in retirement after an active life on the field of battle, finds such minor distractions as the social amenities of the little village and even the pursuit of a wolf or a criminal too lacking in grandeur for his need of domination. As for the queries above, Giono has explained to me that Langlois feels a certain sympathy for the assassin since he shares the same impulse for violence; and the symbolism of the goose blood dropping on the snow, inspired by an episode in Malory's *Morte d'Arthur*, suggests that Langlois chose to take his own life rather than risk the temptation to kill.

In his study of Giono's techniques, to which reference has already been made, Pierre Robert opens an original line of thought in his comparison of Langlois with the Meursault of Camus' *L'Etranger*. Both men find themselves "strangers" in the world about them; but, whereas the hero of Camus is passive and seeks a solution of a metaphysical order, Giono's hero seeks a more concrete solution, a diversion; and, when this fails, he renounces the world through suicide. This act proves, according to Robert, that, for Giono, Langlois ought to submit to the order of things and abandon his pride. But the greatest difference between the two heroes goes deeper than that: "Langlois refuses to believe that he is a stranger. . . . But, refusing to believe himself a stranger, he remains a prey to doubt and this is what will lead him finally to suicide. Langlois appears, therefore, as an anti-Meursault. And his refusal makes him free, up to the moment of his suicide, which he has decided on in full knowledge of the situation, and which makes him enter freely into the order of things." Robert is quite right in calling Langlois the first of Giono's modern heroes; for, though he retains epic qualities such as his kingship (sense of superiority to his fellows), he is modern because he is "sans divertissement."

Among contemporary masters of the novel, Faulkner is doubtless the one whom Giono most admires. Jean Onimus was perhaps the first critic to point out similarities of technique between Faulkner and Giono, particularly in regard to *Un Roi*. As in Faulkner's *Red Leaves* and *Absalom, Absalom!*, the story is told in the first person by individuals in whose obscure interpretation the facts remain suspended: "It is Giono who has succeeded best in France in this type of novel. Giono has not been often enough compared to Faulkner; the resemblances are numerous and profound. In *Un Roi* for example mystery is constantly hovering and the principal character, Langlois, fascinates us up to the end because the drama is apprehended only through the stories of witnesses strung out in time." [4] And Onimus concludes that Giono's heroes are as objective and inviolate as those of Faulkner, for in both cases their gestures are unfolded through the intermediary of witnesses who transmit them, as in a dream, in the climate of a legend.

III Noé

When one asks Giono to name his favorite among his writings, the answer is *Noé* (1947). It is not surprising, therefore, that in 1961 he reissued this, the second volume of his *Chroniques*, which had attracted little notice on its first appearance in 1947. It has often been called "the novelist's novel" because it offers so many insights into the artist's manner of composition. Indeed Pierre Robert has aptly termed it Giono's *Journal des Faux Monnayeurs*. Not truly a novel in the usual sense, its autobiographical character renders it a sort of sequel, conceived in his maturity, to the personal recollections of his boyhood contained in *Jean le bleu*. As for the curious title itself, the most ingenious and plausible explanation has recently been proffered by Robert Kanters. After discussing the period of frustration and misunderstanding through which Giono passed because of the failure of his propaganda mission and his successive imprisonments, Kanters writes: "It is the first word of M. Giono on leaving the ark after a deluge of fire which almost ruined forever his confidence in man and his confidence in his art." Conscious of the necessity to reorient his entire method of composition, "quite rightfully, wishing to write the novelist's novel, he chose for his title the name of the man who one day had to reinvent all by himself the whole of inundated creation." [5]

One is tempted to add that the title might also have been chosen because the book resembles Noah's Ark in the heterogeneous complexity of its contents: the memories which are preserved in this store house from the flood of oblivion. We see Giono in the act of gathering olives from his grove, taking the little train from Manosque to Marseilles, and describing in loving detail the picturesque scenery along the route; then wandering through the narrow streets of the old metropolis in order to reconstruct in his romantic fancy the splendor of the maritime barons a half century before. These promenades give rise to anecdotes, at least two of which—the strange tale of Emperor Jules, who lost his new bride in the fire of the Opera House and was himself reduced to a legless cripple, and the macabre incident of Giono's night in an old ladies' home on the blood-soaked bed of an inmate recently deceased—would be eligible for an anthology of tales of mystery and horror.

More interesting to the student of Giono as a novelist, however, are the glimpses *Noé* affords of his method of composition. Already discussed in earlier chapters of this book were the passages concerning Giono's imprisonment in Fort Saint-Nicolas and the inception of his *Pour saluer Melville.* The first fifty pages of *Noé* are related to the novel he has just finished, *Un Roi sans divertissement,* and possess truly amazing originality. In what has been termed the technique of spatial simultaneousness, Giono confides to us how the characters and scenery of the novel were superimposed in his mind over the walls and surroundings of his own home until true and fictional reality were commingled and coexistent. Pierre Robert has also pointed out another experiment of Giono's *Noé:* his effort to represent temporal simultaneousness in his description of the occupants of his tramway, and their various peregrinations through the streets of the city after leaving the tram. Pierre Robert feels that the new technique, while interesting, is unsuccessful from an esthetic standpoint; for the reader still assigns to their actions the space in time which they receive from the order of the narration. One might add that the artificiality of this method is also apparent because the author is obviously unable in reality to follow his characters once they are out of sight from his position in the tram. But devotees of Giono's later masterpiece *Le Hussard sur le toit* rejoice to meet here for the first time the future hero Angélo as he appeared suddenly to Giono's imagination at the end of a boulevard in Marseilles in the shape of "a rider who seemed like a sheaf of gold on a black horse."

Noé which began with his hallucinating impressions of the novel just completed, concludes with his plans for beginning a new (and up to now unpublished novel) *Les Noces*. At the end, in his discussion of the heroine on the morning of her wedding day, Giono sums up for the reader the essence of his new method of objectivity already foreshadowed in *Un Roi*, which he follows in the remaining *Chroniques*. In regard to her body he writes: "I have the authorization, the right, the duty to describe it entirely. It must be seen. But to describe it as it is on the bed and not as I would see it if I could arrange it at my ease; to put myself at the service of truth; having done this I have the right to invent everything. Soul: to show it through gestures. I am not *inside* this girl, I don't want the reader to be *inside*, I want him to see her as I see her, as if he were the invisible guest at these *Noces*. What he would see then is the comportment of the girl on her bed that morning and it is by the comportment that he would understand in what *état d'âme* she is. This is how I must make her soul understood."

Giono never attains absolute objectivity, and perhaps that is fortunate for his admirers. For it is in this very book, so intimate in its confidences from author to reader, that Giono confesses: "Whatever one does, he always makes the portrait of the Artist by himself. Cézanne—it was an apple of Cézanne."

IV Les Ames fortes

If *Un Roi* was enigmatical and at times frustrating for the reader, *Les Ames fortes* (1949) is even more so. The novel is really a dialogue among several old women who are attending a wake—the nonagenarian Thérèse who tells the story of her life and her sexagenerian comrades who have heard the details from her Aunt Junie and who frequently interrupt Thérèse to give an entirely different version of the same facts. Thérèse herself seems to alter her point of view in the course of the narrative, and it requires great concentration and ingenuity on the part of the reader to reconcile these inconsistencies and to rearrange the chronology. Of all the novels of Giono, *Les Ames fortes* is the one which reminds us most forcibly of Balzac in its blending of exact realism with fantastic melodrama, its hallucinating intensity and its delineation of characters who are all of one piece: they are monsters either of goodness or wickedness. Although the manner of narration prevents Giono from giving vent to any lyric description of nature, the extremely vivid setting affords a striking picture of a little mountain town in the late years of the nineteenth century with its rural industries of lumbering and tanning and its teeming hostelry in which we perceive the bustle of the stage coaches, the cracking of whips, the roaring fire upon the hearth, and the motley procession of travelers. In this milieu the jealousies, cupidities, intrigues, and rivalries of local society are sharply etched. The familiar earthy and slangy expressions of the *langue verte* used by the interlocutors in telling the story help us to accept the strangest adventures as credible.

For Giono, like Balzac, is fascinated by melodrama. What, for instance, could be more melodramatic than the sinister money-lender Reveillard, whose figure casts a baneful shadow over the entire countryside? The plot with Firmin (or is it Thérèse?) by which he schemes in cold blood the financial ruin of the Numance couple would have delighted the creator of *Vautrin* or *César Birotteau*. The dénouement, involving Thérèse's murder of her husband, is likewise fantastic in its sadistic cruelty. Yet, as Nadeau has so shrewdly pointed out, "One could say more justly, although there is indeed something of a Dumas père or Eugène Sue in Giono, that he pushes melodrama to the point where it breaks its moorings." Whereas the spectator of melodrama or the reader of *romans-feuilletons* is interested in the action rather than in the simple and traditional types—the villain, the hero, the victim—here it is the characters which interest us primarily rather than their actions.

The character of Firmin remains a puzzle until the end, for we are left to choose between the contemptible coward and weakling portrayed by his wife Thérèse and the slyly ambitious, unscrupulous villain painted by one of her companions. Giono suggested that both versions are equally true, depending on perspective and point of view of the characters. In spite of the contradictions and overlapping chronology of the conflicting witnesses, the reader realizes that the three main protagonists are aptly called by their author "strong souls"; for they are moved, like Balzacian heroes, by a master passion. M. Numance, benefactor and philanthropist, is really activated less by Christian charity than by his overpowering tenderness for his wife, whose elee-mosynary mania he is happy to indulge. Mme Numance with her aristocratic reserve and delicacy is truly the embodiment of good-ness like Balzac's Cousin Pons, yet she becomes a more human and credible figure if we understand that her love for Thérèse is itself an irresistible passion, subject to jealousy and anxiety, al-most egotistical in its possessiveness. Unlike the victims in Balzac, the Numance couple are highly intelligent, perfectly aware of the traps which are being set for them and which they disdain to evade. When catastrophe comes, they accept it with such indul-gent irony that one can scarcely think of them as victims; for their joy was in giving—and in this sense they have achieved their purpose.

As for Thérèse, she reveals by her own testimony an unforgetta-ble portrait of feminine wickedness worthy to rank beside Balzac's Cousine Bette or Thackeray's Becky Sharp. Conscious of her su-perior intelligence, she avoids the boredom of a small town by practicing hypocrisy until she is able to simulate any quality. Her guile is purely gratuitous since she cares nothing for money or prestige but only for the power of mastery over her victims—her husband, Firmin; her mistress, Mme Numance. In this connection Pierre Robert has been reminded of that other Thérèse who has appeared in several of Mauriac's stories and who is a prey to "the power given her to poison and corrupt." Robert logically con-cludes that both the will to power and the power to poison and corrupt follow an abstract law of fate. The difference, however, between the two heroines of the same name is that Mauriac's Thérèse, like Langlois, is conscious of her condition; Giono's Thérèse is not. Hence she is psychologically less free, "since all freedom implies a state of consciousness." But Thérèse and the other "âmes fortes" in this book "have freedom in the novel in the sense that the author never intervenes; their actions unroll as the logical consequence of their essence." Giono himself has ex-pressed to me his conviction that this freedom left to his charac-ters represents something new in the French novel, and he quoted with approval the statement of one critic that even Giono does not know at the end what his characters will do. In Giono's opinion, this new technique gives his characters greater depth and realism.

On one occasion Thérèse poses an almost impenetrable riddle

for the reader; namely, her frantic despair bordering on temporary insanity at the disappearance of her benefactress. Shall we conclude that this whole episode is merely the crowning touch of her hypocrisy, or shall we infer that unconsciously she has let herself be softened by the love showered upon her. A query put to the author brought forth still another explanation; her anguish is real enough but is caused not by love but by disappointment at seeing her victim escape her. In any case, her subsequent torture and murder of her husband complete a ghastly image of human degradation. At the close of the book, as dawn begins to break, one of the old crones expresses her surprise that, after this sleepless vigil, Thérèse looks fresh as a rose. Never, perhaps, has Giono written anything more savagely sardonic than her reply: "Why would you expect me not to look as fresh as a rose?"

In summary, it may be said that despite our occasional irritation and frustration with Giono's procedure in telling the story, we are held throughout as under a sinister spell and left with an impression of terrifying grandeur. We are tempted to agree with Nadeau: "One should rather envisage *Les Ames fortes* in the perspective of a genre which Giono, as soon as he began to write, wanted to introduce into our epoch: tragedy." Like Greek tragedy, it arouses in us a feeling of "terror and pity." And, if the novel does not possess the pure lines of classical tragedy, it resembles it, according to Nadeau, not only in its plot but also in such characteristics as the chorus and alternating recitals of the various narrators. At any rate, *Les Ames fortes* must be considered one of the most striking and powerful of Giono's *Chroniques*.

V Les Grands Chemins

Les Grands Chemins (1951) forms a distinct contrast with the earlier *Chroniques* in its simplicity of plot and character development, but it is marked by the same new objectivity. It has been compared to the *Novelas Exemplares* of Cervantes and to the *Vida de Lazarillo de Tormès*. It may indeed be classified as a modern version of the picaresque or rogue novel, for the story merely relates the adventures of a wandering couple—the likable vagabond who is the narrator and his friend the despicable Artist, virtuoso not only of the guitar but of cards, of which he manipulates the aces and kings with a mastery of technique which furnishes him a comfortable living. According to Villeneuve, Giono required only five weeks to compose this novel. Perhaps this accounts in part for the fact that it is the weakest and least impressive of the *Chroniques*.

Like so many of Giono's stories, *Les Grands Chemins* is a strange blend of almost banal realism and incredible melodrama. Except for the two catastrophes—the gambler's revenge upon the Artist, and the latter's murder of the old woman and consequent death at the hands of his only friend—the narrative is somewhat monotonous, repetitious, and lackluster. Disillusioned by the failure of the Artist to express any gratitude or warmth of affection, the vagabond ejaculates sadly: "One would say that I am seeing the world for the first time in my life; I look at it, and it bores me. I do not feel any pleasure." For the first time, perhaps, Giono's readers are likely to echo this sentiment. At first, we share with the vagabond his sensuous pleasure in the rich autumnal foliage of the mountainside; but soon the story plunges us into the depressing atmosphere of winter which cloaks the countryside with a uniform blanket of snow over which a murky fog hangs like a pall.

In some respects the vagabond narrator is a thoroughly normal individual, quietly philosophical and skeptical in his even-tempered, common sense approach to life. It is easier for the reader to identify with him than with the Artist who appears to be the central personage. What remains mysterious and elusive in his characterization, however, is his strange attachment to the contemptible Artist, whose unsavory personality he had fathomed at the very outset.

Whatever interest the reader may find in this novel is concentrated primarily in the portrait of the Artist, whose petty knavery is unrelieved by a single redeeming feature. As Pugnet has suggested, he represents in Giono's work a later and more detailed development of an earlier cad, the sinister Louis of *Un de Baumugnes*. The Artist's repulsive physical appearance is in keeping with his crass materialism, and we remember him best for his tendency to slobber in the corner of his mouth at a moment of triumph. A human parasite without a spark of gratitude for his benefactor, frankly preoccupied with the pursuit of gain, the Artist becomes inexplicable only because of his gratuitous murder of the old woman. Perhaps the realization that his beautiful hands, which had performed such marvelous feats of legerdemain, are now crushed and twisted beyond repair, has driven him insane.

Robert suggests here another analogy between Giono and Camus. In Camus' doctrine of the absurd, the only possibility of escape lies in making of one's life a work of art. The Artist had made of his card playing a work of art, the only thing which counted for him in life; "for the artist there is no more reason to live since life has lost its meaning." There is a final bit of irony in the fact that his hands are now too weak even to crush the old woman, who dies from a heart attack. Though the Artist does not actually commit suicide, his death, as Robert points out, "has the quality of suicide" since he does not try to escape and offers no protest to the vengeance of his friend. In any event, the reader—though uncertain whether Giono's central theme is friendship or metaphysical preoccupation with the theory of the absurd—comes, through some alchemy of the author, to share the vagabond's compassion for the wretched creature whose terrible punishment has been so aptly proportioned to his crimes.

VI   Le Moulin de Pologne

The title for *Le Moulin de Pologne* is derived from a country estate that was named, according to tradition, because a Polish pilgrim on his way to Rome once established himself there. The title of the English translation by Peter de Mendelssohn has been changed to the more revealing but less poetic *The Malediction*. If we may believe Villeneuve, the town itself in which much of the action unfolds is a composite of Aix-en-Provence, Sisteron, and Giono's birthplace, Manosque.

The dominant figure in this town is the elegantly dressed and aristocratic M. Joseph, who, despite his fine linen and fashionable attire, lodges for some strange reason with a shoemaker's family in the most plebeian quarter of the town. His antecedents and occupation are unknown, but the respect bordering on fear which he inspires even in the bigwigs of society leads to the rumor that he is really a Jesuit general in civilian disguise. Before the dramatic incident in which he plays the leading role, however, it is necessary for the narrator—an old bachelor lawyer with a rather petty, envious, and materialistic outlook—to trace the tragic story of the Coste family that has been implacably pursued by destiny throughout several generations.

The owner of the estate of the Moulin de Pologne, M. Coste,

after losing his wife and two sons by accidental deaths, had died from blood poisoning caused by an impacted fishhook in his hand; and he had left two beautiful daughters, Clara and Anaïs. Clara was burned to death, along with her husband and two sons, in the wreck of the Paris-Versailles train. Anaïs, whose daughter Marie strangled to death on a cherry stone, died in childbirth that same day, leaving a boy of nine and the baby, Jacques. As Jacques grows to manhood, his elder brother runs away; and his father, after some years of sexual and alcoholic indulgence, has to be placed in an insane asylum. Jacques takes charge of the estate, makes a happy marriage, but dies suddenly at the age of forty-two, leaving a son and daughter, Jean and Julie. Jean, a passionate Don Juan, is found shot to death in the field, apparently by some jealous husband; and later Julie, thrown into convulsions by a shot carelessly fired too close to her ear, recovers, but one side of her face remains horribly distorted while the other side retains the marvelous beauty she had possessed before. It is with this one survivor, Julie, and her marriage with the mysterious M. Joseph that the rest of this story is concerned.

René Lalou has pointed out how skilfully Giono has renewed here in a modern setting the theme of ancient fatality,[6] and Giacomo Antonini has compared the novel to the work of Faulkner for its stark, black atmosphere of mystery and horror.[7] André Rousseaux, always a rather harsh critic of Giono, insists, however, that "this theater of fate reminds one of a little Punch and Judy show in which the puppets disappear whenever it pleases the manipulator. Not for an instant does fate impose a presence of which the mystery would appear to dominate the novelist himself."[8]

As if to forestall criticism that the fatality overhanging his characters is too contrived and persistent to appear natural, Giono has his narrator remark: "I confine myself to telling what I know from reliable sources, and in the simplest possible way." True, the author makes little effort to explain these mysterious happenings, in particular the fantastic and grandiose central episode of the ball, followed by the totally unexpected marriage of M. Joseph with the tragic Julie. Yet, at the same time, our credulity is gained to some extent by the prosaic attitude of the narrator, a most earthy individual who is always citing his sources—individuals or legal documents. We should add likewise that not only are most of the catastrophes natural enough in themselves—the result of an embedded fishhook, a swallowed cherry stone, or a wrecked train—but also the prolongation of this ancestral curse is attributable in part to purely human causes: the suspicious antagonism of the neighbors which drove both Julie and Jean from normality to pathological despair. Interspersed likewise in this skein of nightmarish events is an element of social satire which lashes the petty vanities, jealousies and backbitings of a small town.

Aside from the romantic and poetic figure of Julie, the reader remembers most vividly the mysterious character of the hero, M. Joseph. When Giono was asked why he had not given him any definite profession, such as a banker or magistrate, to explain the awe and veneration of the townspeople, Giono answered with a smile that he had preferred to leave this to the imagination of the reader. This reply furnishes further documentation for Robert's thesis that, in Giono's evolution in the technique of the novel, he is becoming more and more an exponent of the contemporary trend to diminish the role of author and to increase thereby the participation of the reader. Pugnet has asserted that M. Joseph with his impeccable elegance and grace descends like the earlier Langlois directly from the Gonzalès of *Jean le bleu,* but Giono once told me that he had in mind his own father, in whom there was such a blend of benevolence and unfathomed mystery.

Certainly, we find in M. Joseph aspects of the character which had appeared so often in Giono's early works, that of the *guérisseur,* or healer. When the two young heiresses have become objects of public derision because the efforts of their parents to wangle M. Joseph for a son-in-law have ended in palpable failure, it is M. Joseph himself who soothes their vexation by walking publicly with one on each arm. Like so many of Giono's heroes, M. Joseph enjoys to the full the domination he exerts over the local citizenry. Yet, with financial assistance, he is beneficent to all; and he is capable of such ideal love for Julie that all his efforts, whether to enhance his domain or to gather at his mansion the homage of aristocratic society, are directed towards one single purpose: to construct a world of peace and serenity in which she can regain self-confidence and feel secure from the brooding spell of hostile fate.

VII *Evaluation*

In conclusion, it may be said that these *Chroniques,* in spite of wide differences in subject matter, have many distinctive features in common. In each case the story is told in the first person (as so often in Faulkner) by a narrator, usually of ordinary or even subnormal station. As a corollary, the expansive lyricism of Giono is replaced by a simple style, sometimes even slangy and proverbial. In this detachment from his characters, Giono's portraits of human nature are now more objective, ironical, satirical, and disillusioned.

Though Chonez stated that Giono, by his own confession, "has great difficulty in portraying a real scoundrel"—and that he has given us only one example, the narrator of *Le Moulin de Pologne,* (who is vulgar and petty but scarcely wicked)—she has forgotten the savage murderer of *Un Roi,* the avaricious Firmin and hypocritical Thérèse of *Les Ames fortes,* and trickster L'Artiste of *Les Grands Chemins.* Surely these are enough to form a respectable rogue's gallery for any author!

In each of these books one finds the same mingling of minute realism with fantastic adventures for which the explanation is often left to the reader's imagination. And, finally, all of the *Chroniques* present heroes who have indomitable energy and vitality; who are more imagined than observed; who are moved in most cases by a single passion, that of domination; and whose mysterious actions in a magic world of romantic melodrama hold the reader as in a trance.

CHAPTER 16

The Hussard Cycle

I *Subjectivity*

FROM time to time during the composition of his post-war chronicles Giono has returned with filial piety to the series of novels whose chief protagonists exemplify members of his own family—his grandfather, the Italian carbonaro; his father; and his mother. Unequal though these volumes may be in literary merit, they possess in common the unique interest of being the most personal of his works, the ones in which his own background, affections, and aspirations are most clearly discernible. When *Pauline* appears as the last of the six volumes in the Hussard Cycle, Giono plans to publish them all in one huge volume, not in the order of their publication but in accordance with the chronology of the action. In anticipation of this development, it seems best to follow the same arrangement in this discussion.

II L'Ecossais

L'Ecossais (1955) is probably the least known of Giono's works since it has not yet been made available to the general public. The circumstances of its publication for sale by the Rotary Club of Manosque as a philanthropic project will be related in the following chapter. Printed on vellum and boxed in a limited edition of eighteen hundred copies, with *lettrines* and *culs de lampe* representing woodcuts of the seventeenth century and with *bandeau* by the artist Lucien Jacques, this exquisite volume is now a collector's item.

While the author does not mention the exact date of the events in *L'Ecossais*, internal evidence seems to place it in the 1830's during the reign of the Orléanist king, Louis Philippe, shortly before the incidents described in *Angélo*. As so often is the case in the *Chroniques*, the tale is related by a participant—in this case, an officer of the constabulary called to investigate a savage crime, the ambush of a stagecoach on the road from Aix to Nice with the murder of all the occupants including coachman, postilion, and three travelers. Even more shocking had been the treatment accorded to the military guard, Lieutenant Brigon, whose head had been crushed under three stones.

Setting out in a snow storm with his brigade of fifteen men to comb the desolate mountain country from which the bandits must have come, Captain Martial discovers a woman's sweater entangled in a bush and becomes convinced that it has some relation to the crime. Leaving his men behind him, he proceeds fearlessly to the tiny hamlet of Barjaux near the scene of the ambush, but he finds it deserted save for one house with a faint light showing in the window. Upon knocking, he is admitted by an elderly lady who leaves him in the presence of a beautiful young woman in elegant attire. When we read that her face is "en fer de lance," we realize at once that she is none other than Pauline de Théus who occupies so important a rôle throughout the cycle. When Martial hands her the sweater, she frankly acknowledges it as her own; for she had deliberately left it as a decoy to attract him here.

She explains that her band of Legitimist sympathizers had attacked the royal Orléanist coach and that the apparently wanton slaughter was really the result of a pitched battle. However, an unknown member of the attackers, infuriated by the resistance of Lieutenant Brigon, had ignobly avenged himself by crushing the guard's head with rocks, thereby bringing shame upon all the Legitimist faction. She calls upon Martial, therefore, to act as an impartial judge and to accept as expiation the execution of the chief, the elderly Marquis de Théus, her husband. The Marquis now enters with his companion and guest, the Scotchman Macdui, who is on his way from Edinburgh to Frascati to pay homage to the last lineal descendant of the Stuarts, Cardinal Henri Benôit. Macdui asserts that, just as the name of the Duke of Cumberland has remained an object of contempt among the Scots because of the cruel massacre he commanded at Culloden, so the Marquis and his partisans will be unable to live down the disgrace for the base treatment of Lieutenant Brigon until they are purged by a voluntary sacrifice.

Pauline now pleads with Captain Martial to shoot her instead of her husband, but he decides that death is an insufficient expiation—the murderers must live with their shame. As Captain Mar-

tial is mounting his horse, he hears a pistol shot: The Scotsman
has offered himself as a gratuitous victim whom Martial is forced
to accept. The final ironic touch is the discovery that the papers of
state which Lieutenant Brigon had been told to defend with his
life were only dummies.

The subtitle of *L'Ecossais* is *La Fin des Héros*. Its glorification
of the *point d'honneur* reminds one of Mérimée's *Partie de Tric-
trac* which it resembles also in its military conciseness and matter-
of-fact tone—a style that serves by its very understatement to render the catastrophe more poignant. When Giono was questioned
concerning this analogy, he replied, however, that his memory of
Mérimée's story was blurred by the fact that twenty years had
elapsed since his reading; but he confirmed the suggestion that
Mérimée is one of his favorite authors, particularly for the *Corre-
spondance*.

III Angélo

Angélo first appeared as a serial in *La Nouvelle Revue
Française* in 1953, in German translation the same year, and
finally in book form in France in 1958. Yet Giono tells us in the
Preface that it was composed in six days in Marseilles in 1938, not
as a finished novel but as a sort of preliminary exercise for *Le
Hussard* in order to analyze the personality of his hero and to
observe his reactions in regard to two women—the actress Anna
de Clèves; and the Marchioness, Pauline de Théus. "This text is
therefore a simple laboratory report. It was a question not of composition but of experimentation." With an author as subtle and
mystificateur as Giono, it is sometimes dangerous to take his asser-
tions too literally, as we have seen in the case of his translation of
Moby Dick. Though *Angélo* is far from being a perfected masterpiece like *Le Hussard* and ends abruptly as if the author had been
interrupted before finishing his tale, this slender volume nevertheless has such literary merit and charm that it seems inconceivable
it could have been dashed off so swiftly.

The story opens with the arrival of young Colonel Angélo Pardi
in Briançon as a fugitive from his native Piedmont where he had
killed in a duel the hated Austrian spy, Baron Schwartz. (Like
Giono's grandfather, the famous carbonaro, Angélo appears in
full-dress uniform and cavalry saber). Changing to the white cor-
duroy costume of a laborer in order to proceed unmolested to the

post-chaise in Gap, Angélo is offered a lift by the elderly Marquise de Théus, whom he then accompanies in the stagecoach from Gap to Aix; saves from the attack of horsemen who ambush the coach; and conducts safely to the château of her brother, the Marquis de Théus. As their guest in a pavilion near the château, Angélo is fascinated by the exquisite perfume emanating from a little handkerchief he finds in a porcelain vase. When sent to Aix with a message for the vicar-general, ostensibly in regard to a long distance chess game, he takes with him the precious scented handkerchief whose possessor he hopes some day to encounter.

Provided by the vicar-general with a fashionable costume, a sword, and an attractive apartment, Angélo becomes so adept at fencing that he arouses the admiration of all the young ladies of Aix, with one of whom, the actress Anna de Clèves, he carries on a tender flirtation. When he receives an invitation to return as guest to the château, he meets Pauline, the young wife of the Marquis, who rather naïvely expresses her admiration for Angélo's manly vigor and chivalric grace. Just as the reader is beginning to fear (or hope) that there will soon be a *ménage à trois*, Angélo is sent away by the Marquis on a dangerous mission; and the novel ends in a most unexpected fashion.

Though descriptive passages are minimized, as in most of Giono's later work, one finds nonetheless the familiar atmosphere of strangeness and mystery inherent in all his *Chroniques*. Most of the characters who become prominent in the major volumes of the cycle are already adumbrated here. Though she enters the story only through her correspondence, we meet Angélo's energetic and passionate mother, the Duchess d'Ezzia. Rarely has Giono created a more striking personage than the old Marquise de Théus, faithful after forty years to the memory of her profligate husband whom she calls endearingly "Diablon" and with whose spirit she communes from her armchair while her rooms are ablaze with candelabra as on the occasion when she saw him enter for the first time. Yet her tender heart is hidden from the world by a brusque frankness of speech and a sharp, almost masculine business sagacity.

The most appealing section of the novel is the first meeting of the old marchioness with her new sister-in-law Pauline and the latter's avowal of her love and admiration for her husband the Marquis, almost fifty years her senior. His bravery and nobility of soul she has grown to appreciate during his long months of convalescence at her home after his life had been saved by her father, the doctor; the latter represents one more example in Giono of the healer or *guérisseur* based on memories of his father. And, finally, Angélo himself is introduced to the reader much as he appears in later volumes—young, intrepid, high-spirited, quick-tempered, aristocratic. He is possessed above all with a delicate sense of honor, a striving for the sublime and a distaste for all that is base and sordid.

IV Le Hussard sur le toit

Of all his novels published since the war, *Le Hussard sur le toit* (1951) has been the most universally acclaimed. Marcel Arland, for instance, feels that it dominates Giono's new works even more than *Le Chant du monde* does his earlier ones. "It is a novel in which the former poet and the new narrator join hands." [1] Walter Orlando recognizes in the author "the silhouette of the first contemporary novelist. One finds again the wingèd tone of the great story tellers." [2] Dominique Aury finds the novel "luxuriant and compact, without loss of poetic radiance or clarity." [3] The London *Times Literary Supplement* is greatly impressed: "With *Le Hussard* and its successor *Angélo* Giono has stridden forward with a giant's step. He reveals himself as one of the most important novelists in Europe today." [4] Mario Maurin finds *Le Hussard* vastly superior to *La Peste* of Camus[5]; and even Rousseaux, long the most acerbic critic of Giono, praises *Le Hussard* if only to point out thereby his distaste for Giono's earlier work.[6] The only slightly discordant note in this paean of praise is that of Professor Peyre, who has written so enthusiastically of Giono's earlier manner; but even Peyre tempers his restrictions by calling *Le Hussard* "one of the most youthful and freshest novels of the last fifteen years."

The effect of the story of *Le Hussard* on the reader is paradoxical in the extreme. Never has Giono painted a more somber, ghastly fresco than in these realistic scenes of devastation and horror caused by the cholera—scenes made even more terrifying by the quiet objectivity with which they are related. Almost equally sadistic are the actions of most of the inhabitants, whose superstitious credulity and egotistic concentration on self-preservation lead them to acts of savagery and baseness. On the other hand, the nobility, charm, good humor, and courage of the hero

Angélo are so infectious that the reader, far from feeling depressed, is left with an impression of buoyant optimism. Orlando expressed the judgement of all the critics when he wrote: "From the sea to the Alps, it is a stairway of corpses. Yet the book is bathed in a truly solar happiness . . . . one comes out of it with exaltation." The reason for this paradoxical reaction on the part of the reader is perhaps best pointed out by Maurice Thiébaut: "After all, to show that by abnegation and courage one can safeguard the enjoyment of happiness in the midst of the worst disasters seems to me more useful than the enterprise of philosopher-novelists who seek to draw contrary conclusions from analogous circumstances." [7]

If *Le Hussard* has been the most successful of Giono's post-war novels, just as *Le Chant du monde* was for his earlier period, the explanation in both cases is the same: the perfect balance he has achieved among his various gifts as descriptive artist, narrator, and creator of character. While the lyric descriptions of nature exist in *Le Hussard* not for their own sake but to set the mood for the action, the picturesque background of upper Provence is constantly before us with its panorama of peaceful valleys and rounded hills; its fields of lavender; its gloomy, solitary forests; and, ever in the distance, the purple mountains of the Alps. Usually these descriptions are sober and restrained, the only exception being those of the opening pages in which the silver pallor of the scorching sun, the stifling heat, the parched hillsides, and the shriveled foliage create an atmosphere of burning thirst and tragic foreboding for the scenes of pestilence about to enfold.

Unlike his procedure in earlier books, Giono, during the eight years consumed in writing *Le Hussard*, submitted himself to the most rigorous documentation; he studied the medical records of the departments involved and consulted with doctors concerning the technical aspects of cholera. Nevertheless, in spite of the realism of detail, the plague seems an element of nature, an epic force which, like a gigantic tidal wave, sweeps throughout this vast region from the Mediterranean to the Alps—and mocks the puny efforts of mere mortals to arrest its awesome progress. To quote Thiébaut once more: "*Le Hussard* is above all the epic of cholera. Cholera is the great personage of this work, and I mean not an allegory but a being, most alive and fecund."

Never has the imagination of Giono shown itself to be more

fertile in the invention of dramatic incidents and he has resolved successfully the seemingly impossible task of describing a thousand victims while avoiding the pitfall of monotony and repetition. The critic Aury may have been carried away by his fulsome admiration, but his reaction differs only in degree from his fellow reviewers: "the narrative has become as natural as the respiration of a teller of the thousand and one nights, or of a Greek rhapsody, or of a reciter of *chansons de geste*. For it is indeed of the epic that one thinks constantly, in regard to this inexhaustible inspiration, so direct and continually reborn."

As in all epics, the protagonists are creatures of heroic stature. Undaunted by the dangers confronting him from pestilence and human wickedness, Angélo Pardi rides serene, clad, like a medieval Galahad, in the shining armor of his honor; and he is like Lancelot in his chivalrous protection of the gentler sex. Yet Angélo somehow remains fascinatingly human in his ingenuous vanity, in his constant fear of becoming a laughing-stock because of his tender years, in his remorse for having abandoned the corpse of the heroic doctor who haunts his memory henceforth as "le petit Français," in his probing self-analysis to determine whether he is really motivated by a love for liberty or only by the thrill of adventure. In Giono's frequent use of the "interior monologue" to bring forth various facets of his hero, we are reminded of Stendhal, whose influence is still more evident in the sequel. Because of Giono's successful employment of this technique, Pierre Robert finds Angélo the most outstanding of all of Giono's characters—and, incidentally, the one who resembles Giono the most, or perhaps rather Giono as he would like to be, just as Fabrice is the ideal of Stendhal.

Pauline, Marquise de Théus, is a worthy companion for Angélo. Devoted to her sexagenarian husband whom she admires for his rugged courage and grandeur of resolution, she shows herself to be fearless and indefatigable despite her delicate figure and her slender face *"en fer de lance."* In the depths of her large green eyes lies a suggestion of mystery which enhances her poetic charm. Several critics have been astonished by the total absence between the marquise and Angélo of amorous passion throughout their long cavalcade together. Apparently it would have been naïve to account for this lack through Pauline's sense of fidelity to her aged spouse. It may be of interest to know that Giono himself explains this phenomenon by the psychological state created in both protagonists because of the presence of so many corpses; he adds wryly that his study of population statistics during the cholera epidemic of 1838 showed a striking decrease in natality.

Among the minor characters, Angélo's mother, Duchess d'Ezzia, who appears only through a long letter but who is developed in the sequel *Le Bonheur fou,* reminds one of Fabrice's aunt in *La Chartreuse de Parme.* Adventuresome and passionate, she counsels her son to throw prudence to the winds in his quest for fame and glory. His foster brother Giuseppe, who admires Angélo fanatically yet chides him for risking his life in an honorable duel when he could have accomplished the same result through a hired assassin, is, like Sancho Panza, a sort of foil or echo in a lower key to this modern Don Quixote. "Le petit Français," the heroic young doctor, appears all too briefly, but Angélo's ever-present memory of him relieves somewhat the atmosphere of human depravity which pervades the story. Equally heroic in her own way is the fantastic figure of the nun in Manosque. With her ungainly appearance, her massive hands and feet, and her simple-minded earthiness, she is a grotesque, comic character. Of the plague victims whose bodies she washed, she said simply: "They are my clients, I am responsible for them. On the day of Resurrection, they will be clean." Her consternation when one of these corpses suddenly comes to life and reproaches her for his nudity is an example of the *humour noir* which helps to keep the narrative from becoming too oppressive. There are countless other characters in *Le Hussard* who take on life and verisimilitude though they are glimpsed only briefly.

V   Le Bonheur fou

Just as Giono had sorted out police reports and medical statistics about cholera for his *Hussard,* so, before writing its sequel, he had documented himself on the Italian Revolution of 1848 by scanning the memoirs of Gavone, a lieutenant in the Bes brigade deployed around Peschiera, and also the six thick volumes of the historian Pardi. As a tribute of gratitude to the latter, he has given the name of Pardi to his hero Angélo for a family name.

Le Bonheur fou (1957) is, therefore, an historical novel that portrays the abortive rebellion of the Italian states against Austrian domination in 1848. After a very long and tedious chapter in which the background of the revolution is somewhat cryptically discussed, the reader is plunged into the atmosphere of this stirring age in which dazzling glimpses of Italian lakes, valleys, and mountainsides in the springtime alternate with scenes of carnage in the narrow Milan streets or of the epic disarray of Italian armies driven by the Austrians across the Mincio. Because of the ever-present irony of the author, this colorful pageant of kings and dukes, Napoleonic generals, and noble ladies, wily innkeepers, and saucy serving maids, seems less an assemblage of flesh-and-blood characters than figures out of an Italian opera who strut theatrically across the stage.

In the English translation, the title has been changed to *The Straw Man;* for the hero Angélo has been designated by shrewd conspirators to become a sort of glorious sacrifice in order to arouse the patriotic fervor of the masses in revolt. As a straw man whose destiny is to be burned, all that is asked of him by the cold-blooded plotter Bondino is "to make a lot of smoke under cover of which we can get to work." Unaware at first of these Machiavellian machinations, Angélo nevertheless emerges unscathed from duels, secret missions, pitched battles, and ambushes because of his naïveté, his sense of honor, and his admirable dexterity with saber, musket, or bayonet. The original French title with its reminiscence of Stendhal fits the novel better, for Angélo with his vivacious charm and with his quest for glory and happiness reminds us at once of Fabrice, hero of *La Chartreuse de Parme.*

In contrast to their reception of *Le Hussard,* the attitude of most critics towards *Le Bonheur fou* was one of consternation in which disillusionment and perplexity alternated. Many of them, like Maurice Thiébaut, dismissed it as a mere pastiche of Stendhal's *Chartreuse de Parme* which it resembles in the dry conciseness of style (Orlando had made an untranslatable pun when he asked the reader to notice "le léger beylement"); in Angélo's resemblance to Fabrice; and in the similarity of scenes reuniting for the last time Angélo with his mother, Fabrice with Clélia. Gaëtan Picon agrees that Giono's renunciation in *Le Bonheur* of his usual sustained development and lyricism removes the last obstacles to the influence of Stendhal, which is apparent here in the brief interior monologues ("Suis-je heureux?"), the theme of happiness and liberty, and the blend of generosity and irony. Yet Picon advises those who reproach Giono for giving a mere pastiche of Stendhal to look more deeply into the work: "If Giono borrows from Stendhal, it is not to remake him. Perhaps it is to unmake him, or rather to find again some of his virtues on a quite different plane." [8] In the same article Picon disposes of the absurd charge that, under the guise of innocent diversion, Giono had mounted an attack against the Resistance and the Liberation.

Other than a certain similarity and lack of depth in the characters, the feature which has disconcerted most critics of *Le Bonheur* is the rapid, discontinuous style. Mario Maurin, for instance, compares Giono's overindulgence in ellipses to a sort of Saint Vitus' dance and asks sarcastically, "Why this mad urge for speed. One doesn't take an airplane to cross the street." [9] Gaëtan Picon, keener than other critics in penetrating Giono's intentions in this work, has given the answer. Justifying this new explosive style of discontinuity and dispersion as being in accord with the book's theme of wandering, adventure, chance, and of happiness entrusted to the moment, Picon realizes that Giono is experimenting with a new style—just as for thirty years he has been constantly renewing himself, refusing his own imitation: "In appearance the book bears the colors of Stendhal—or of Walter Scott. In reality it is much closer to the most noteworthy experiments of the modern novel." The real problem which Giono has attempted to solve in *Le Bonheur fou* is this: how can a contemporary style of narration be introduced into the conventions of the novel, how can our shattered, atomized conception of man and time be related to the pleasures of the imagination? "*Le Bonheur fou* is an experimental novel in which experimentation seeks the survival of the old romantic charm." In the meantime, as we read the book, if we can no longer abandon ourselves to a beautiful river, if we are upset by each short wave, "it behooves us to find again little by little the movement of these thwarted waters, the pleasure of their oscillation."

Giono himself with his fondness for mystification must have been amused by the efforts of critics to discover his real purpose in writing *Le Bonheur fou*. Most ingenious among these seekers is Luccioni who has discussed and abandoned various false leads: glorified Western in which "the reader would gladly ascribe to Angélo the head of Gary Cooper"; detective novel; novel of realism; novel of chivalry. This last hypothesis seems to Luccioni entirely plausible, for this novel is obviously a pilgrimage to his ancestors, particularly the carbonaro grandfather; and Giono's veneration for his family makes him necessarily a chevalier: "*Le Bonheur fou* is certainly not the quest for the Holy Grail; but it is a sort of *Orlando Furioso*. Giono rejects the Christian-chivalric tradition, but he rediscovers with delight the pseudo-chivalric poem or Ariosto, to whom he so often refers." [10] With some shrewdness, however, Luccioni concludes that *Le Bonheur fou* is primarily none of these things but rather a prodigious *étude* in which Giono, musician that he is, has given free rein to experimentation with his Paganini-like virtuosity.

It seems incontrovertible that Luccioni and Picon are justified in their surmise that Giono has attempted here something entirely new in his manner of writing. He confided to me that he is more nearly satisfied with *Le Bonheur fou* than with anything else he has composed. When asked why each character other than the hero drops out of sight before we have an opportunity to become attached to him, Giono replied that this was to emphasize the solitude of the hero. When questioned, perhaps rather tactlessly, why he had made the mistake of including the long first chapter with its sixty pages of complicated historical background, which taxes the reader's patience before the story proper commences with Angélo's entrance, his reply was unexpectedly frank: "You are quite right; I think exactly as you do." Then he explained that he had originally intended to put this material in an appendix and will omit it in the one-volume version of the entire cycle. Giono is quick to recognize that *Le Bonheur fou* with its concise style has "dérouté le lecteur," but he remains quite unperturbed, confident that fifty years from now this will be the most widely read of all his books. When reminded that a famous author of whom he is very fond once uttered a similar prophecy, he did not seem displeased by the comparison.

VI Pauline

Though *Pauline* is not yet scheduled for publication, Giono has already completed the main outline and has been kind enough to furnish a summary of the action. After the end of *Le Bonheur fou* Pauline's husband, the elderly Marquis de Théus, dies; and she comes to Italy to look for Angélo. His mother tells Pauline of the duel between Angélo and Giuseppe which resulted in the latter's death; but she is without news of her son who left for France to seek Pauline, and she thinks he must be dead. Pauline, however, is certain that Angélo is still alive; she feels that she would have had a premonition of his death. The Duchess suggests, therefore, that they set out in search for Angélo, taking with them as "chiens de chasse" the other two women who also love Angélo: Lavinia, Giuseppe's widow who constantly adored Angélo; and the old nurse who has always loved him possessively. Each one obtains news of Angélo's whereabouts; but, through jealousy, each causes him to escape so that the others will not find him. Finally, however, Pauline discovers Angélo and hides him in a place where he will be safe just for her.

The subject of the novel is not love but "la recherche de l'amour." Written in a style full of tenderness, quite different from that of *Le Bonheur*, the novel is entirely concerned with feminine protagonists, just as *Le Bonheur* was altogether masculine. Angélo himself never appears in person though his shadow is ever present.

VII Mort d'un personnage

Curiously enough this final volume in the Hussard saga was the first to be published (1949). The story is narrated in the first person by young Angélo Pardi, grandson of Pauline, Marquise de Théus. At the opening of the novel, young Angélo's father, who bears the same name and is the illegitimate son of Pauline and Colonel Angélo Pardi, is director of an asylum for the blind in Marseilles. Pauline at the age of seventy-five has sold her magnificent Château de la Vallette and with the bags of gold realized from the transaction has come to live with her son and grandson in this institution. Still beautiful and aristocratic with her lovely silvered hair, she lives in a strange world of her own, thinking only of the lover she had lost so long ago. Sometimes she makes a circle with her hands on the forehead of her grandson who looks more like the Hussard than does her own son; sometimes in the night she comes to her grandson's door, calling "Angélo, Angélo"; but he remains silent rather than disillusion her with reality.

Some fifteen years later young Angélo returns from naval service to find his father occupying a small, three-room apartment with the nonagenarian Pauline, now deaf, blind, and bedridden. It is strange to see this haughty aristocrat, previously so detached from mundane cares in her absorption with the past, evincing

now an almost childish interest in food and sweets. The details of
her last illness and death have a distressing realism which is however ennobled and rendered intensely moving by the patience and
devotion of her grandson who realizes that he must now love his
grandmother for herself, not for himself, until his new love becomes "radiant, glacial and more sparkling than hoarfrost."

Mort d'un personnage has received less attention from critics
than any other major work of the *Chroniques*. Thoroughly unfavorable was the impression it made on Jean Larnac who deemed
it "A novel without great interest, written in a school boy's
style." [11] He finds the descriptions flat, useless, and redundant and
is moved only by the final pages "when the grandson lovingly
bathes the impotent grandam. There is certainly something atro-
ciously poignant there." Yet Larnac considers that a short story
would have been sufficient to evoke what Shakespeare evoked
with two lines in *As You Like It*. On the other hand, Louis
Chaigne praises the work for having attained "a kind of vesperal
solemnity, a starkness, a sobriety which one would never have
thought possible with Giono." [12]

Most enthusiastic is Claudine Chonez who considers that the
two portraits of love which Giono has painted—that of Mme
Numance for Thérèse (*Les Ames fortes*) and that of little Angélo
for his grandmother—are

two summits of his work. One sees there the freest gift of oneself puri-
fied until it becomes a sort of absolute serenity in which the ego no
longer counts. There is something miraculous in the crystalline sound
which these pages make, when one realizes that Giono spares us no
sordid description and that it is continually a question of bathing a
soiled old body and of handing nourishment to a toothless mouth,
twisted by greediness. All of that—magnified by the love which is
able to see there a trace of pristine grandeur—undergoes a transfiguration without equal, I believe, in all French fiction.

From a purely technical aspect, Pierre Robert finds that Giono has
made progress in this novel over his earlier work, particularly in
his use of the grandson as narrator. He is certainly the one best
qualified to tell the story; and, since the central interest is not
concentrated on him, this fact leaves a certain freedom of movement between author and chief protagonist. Furthermore, "the
tone of the novel is much less impersonal with a narrator speaking

in the first person—and the subject itself demands a tone which is not impersonal."

The majestic figure of Pauline, the aged marchioness, dominates the book as she does all those around her with her beauty, grace, dignity, and evocation of tragic mystery. There is a fascinating contrast between the eyes of the blind patients, dull and glassy yet still turning with excited animation towards the sounds and odors of daily existence, and the great, green eyes of the Marquise, who seemed to look past reality towards a distant world which her companions were powerless to fathom: "This absence in her glance does not mean that she had no color in her eyes. On the contrary she had immense eyes with a very beautiful color. This radiant color, a dark green all threaded with gold, rested on you. It was not a physical absence which astonished you in these eyes; it was an absence of soul . . . that was as definitely separated from you as the soul of a slab of porphyry or onyx."

In the character of her son Angélo Pardi, director of the asylum, Giono has once more paid tribute to his father. His first act as administrator was to remove the blind patients from damp, gloomy quarters to the warm, sunlit third floor, though he had to take out of his own salary the six hundred francs a year formerly paid to the asylum by the commercial renters of this space. When his mother expresses the desire to have her money evaporate in smoke, he is happy to spend it to improve the daily fare of his wards. Reduced to poverty in his retirement, he nevertheless manages to keep always on hand a supply of pastries and bonbons to gratify the craving of the nonagenarian.

The atmosphere of gloom of this novel is somewhat relieved by picturesque descriptions of the teeming, narrow streets of Marseilles with their exotic colors and pungent odors, and by the comic figure of "pauvre fille," the servant girl who takes young Angélo to school every morning but who is always so tipsy by evening that it is the little child who must lead her back to the asylum. A volume which begins in an institution for the blind and ends with a deathbed agony may seem, however, a rather depressing finale for the epic cycle of the Hussard. Yet no novel in the series is written with greater emotion or tenderness. Just as the dashing figure of Colonel Angélo Pardi in the earlier volumes was inspired by Giono's swashbuckling carbonaro grandfather, the Pauline of this book represents a moving tribute to his mother, whose name was also Pauline and whose long illness and death inspired that of her namesake in *Mort d'un personnage*. As Giono wrote on the flyleaf of my copy, this is the book "which has counted most in my life since I have expressed in it the death of my mother." Giono's filial pilgrimage to the memory of his ancestors is now complete.

CHAPTER 17

Honors and New Horizons

I *Prize Winner and Academician*

THE last decade and a half have brought Giono increasing recognition as one of the truly great personalities and creators of contemporary France. And the prospect of advancing age has brought no terrors for Giono. In an interview in 1954[1] Giono optimistically declared: "Old age is a beautiful period. Fewer cares and impatiences, more experience and finesse in the art of enjoying things." Similarly, the following year he insisted to Christian Millau[2] that "Sixty years is middle age. In my country one is young until ninety-two. After that one begins to grow old." The secret of his happiness is divulged in the rest of the interview: "I have just had two hundred rose bushes planted under my window; that is true happiness. The most beautiful sky in France, five little Brazilian cigars every day, a little bit of *Don Quixote* or of Machiavelli, a letter of Stendhal, a glass of cool water, a few measures of Scarlatti, a passage from Mozart's *Don Giovanni* and my work table—it doesn't take any more than that to have made me, for forty years, happy as the full moon and tranquil as a jar of oil, constantly, minute by minute." His only worries during this period were frequent attacks of arthritis and gout, which he called "attacks of acute injustice" and which now seem much improved.

Though Giono does not mention it, it is unlikely that the external honors which have come to him in this period could have failed to enhance his satisfaction. As early as 1952 *Carrefour* wondered if Giono was the greatest novelist of our time; and *Paris Match* nominated Giono's *Moulin* for the Grand Prix of Venice of the international novel, bringing loud outcries from the pro-Communist *Lettres Françaises*. Next came the Prix Monégasque. In 1950 Prince Rainier of Monaco had founded a prize of one million francs for the best ensemble of works by an author in the French language. Despite the efforts of Duhamel, who presided over the jury in the absence of Prince Rainier, to give the honor to his candidate Henri Bosco, Giono was awarded the prize for 1953.

In the autumn of 1954 Giono was persuaded by Gérard Bauër to present his candidacy for the seat vacated by the death of Colette at the Académie Goncourt. For months before the election there had been impassioned discussion of favored candidates, among them Sartre, Malraux, Jean Reverdy, and Giono. Because the vacant seat had belonged to a woman, many held that Existentialist Simone de Beauvoir, or some other female writer, should be chosen. Jean Giono was elected. After that it was only an anticlimax and a foregone conclusion to learn that Mlle de Beauvoir had received the annual Goncourt prize for her latest novel, *Les Mandarins*.

II *Machiavelli*

As early as 1950, while still in the midst of his *Chroniques,* Giono had become fascinated by the enigmatic personality of Machiavelli. A study of his Correspondence in the library of the Vatican at Rome convinced him that only a small proportion of these letters had been published and that even these had been distorted in the French translation. In an article in the October, 1951, number of *La Table Ronde* Giono took issue with the prevailing reputation of Machiavelli by portraying him as an estimable character in private life, fond of simple country scenes and pleasures, faithful to his friends and totally lacking in arrogance or pride.

The following year saw the appearance of Giono's *Introduction to the Complete Works of Machiavelli* (*Introduction aux oeuvres complètes de Machiavel*) presented by M. Edmond Barincou. Giono's essential preoccupation in this important essay is to convince us that Machiavelli has a message for our own time. In Giono's eyes, the originality of the Renaissance resided in its endeavor to see things as they really are and not through the illusion of Christianity: "Machiavelli is concerned only with the sad truth. It is on this basis that he is a modern writer. Since Machiavelli's purpose is to determine whether it is possible for man to govern man, he is logically drawn therefore to the study of man, in which he shows himself a master. *The Prince* might well be titled 'Ambition.' *The History of Florence* can be read like a novel for the masses, written by a profound psychologist." Giono insists that Machiavelli's man is not the villain of a Shakespeare or of a Marlowe but any man "who has accepted the principle that the material world perceived by our senses is the only reality and that outside this reality there is nothing. It is the man of today." And Giono finds at every moment in *The History of Florence* the tone of our daily newspaper and in the *Discourses* the language of our radio broadcasts.

According to Giono, we shall not find in Machiavelli any political doctrine but only "an understanding of the human heart, unveiled in an ensemble of principles which are political only because they are general." In his evaluation of the value of man, Machiavelli is less interested in formulating moral judgments than in the motivation common to all. Giono finds Machiavelli's to be the first and perhaps the only purely objective examination of man: "the study of passions made dispassionately, like the study of a problem in mathematics; an essential preoccupation with precision and truth; an absolute rejection of anything which would have to be accepted without proof."

The reader will recall, in connection with Giono's treatment of Melville, his tendency to identify the subject of his study with himself. Here too it is instructive to observe Giono's effort to draw Machiavelli closer to him: "It is not a question of the happiness of humanity in Machiavelli; it is only a question of personal happiness. He is not a misanthropist; he is a *bon vivant.*" Admitting that Machiavelli seems to have lived through the glorious period of painting and sculpture without having been artistically moved by them (Giono has often deprecated his own understanding of art though he helped gain recognition for his friend Bernard Buffet), Giono rejoices nevertheless that both he and Machiavelli belong to the "civilization of olive oil" and that, unlike Hobbes, the Italian writer gives us many descriptions of nature. "A little stilted, stuffed with kings, popes and peoples but logical and precise as a peasant in his vineyard, astride his horse, Machiavelli composes the Georgics of modern times."

In spite of his enthusiasm for the great Florentine, Giono admits that his poetry is second-rate; but he finds him a good dramatist and praises his prose style which makes his tales as good as the *Decameron.* Calling him "a professor of energy" in his works as well as in his life, Giono would like to apply to him the motto *"servire"* which is found in the margin of Leonardo da Vinci's most beautiful sketches; "good servant" ought to be Machiavelli's epitaph.

Perhaps the Italian critic Spaziani is justified in feeling that Giono's interpretation is too tendenciously modern and that the spiritual affinity derived from the participation of both writers in the "civilization of olive oil" is rather a gastronomic one. In his reaction to Giono's assertion that Machiavelli has given us "the Georgics of modern times" and that some of his texts afford us a humor à la Swift, Spaziani also expresses great reserve concerning the "logical and constructive faculty" of the brilliant French political dilettante.[3]

III   *Foreign Travel*

In the spring of 1953 accompanied by his elder daughter Aline, Giono made a trip to the Cumberland and English lake country, which he found somewhat spoiled by tourism, and then to the Scottish border, where he was enchanted by the fidelity to traditions of the past represented by the presence of kilts and bagpipes with ribbons indicating the colors of the clan. So charmed was he with the warmth and friendliness he found in Scotland that he remarked: "If I should ever leave Manosque, it is in the neighborhood of Inverness that I would go to live." When he wrote the next year the novelette *L'Ecossais* (The Scotsman), the mention of Culloden and the heroic episode of the Highlander were no doubt inspired by this journey.

The year 1953 was one of unusual traveling for the hitherto sedentary novelist, for in September he set out with his wife and two friends in the tiny "Quatre Chevaux" (4CV) across the pass of Mont-Genèvre to tour northern Italy. His purpose was to see the landscapes of Tuscany, Lombardy, and Venetia that were already familiar to him from the reading of Italian authors. No less influential was his desire to know the country of his famous grandfather, the carbonaro outlaw (and incidentally, perhaps, of his other grandfather, the French zouave who took part in the Battle of Magenta). Not long before, Giono had completed his *Hussard*, whose shadow went with him everywhere as he imagined the places in which his hero would have the experiences described later in its sequel, *Le Bonheur fou*.

Yet more important, perhaps, than any of these motives was the simple pleasure to be found in travel itself, for Giono states frankly: "Is it necessary to say that I did not come here to know Italy but to be happy." This happiness is experienced by Giono individually not in the presence of landmarks most often praised by tourists and travelogues but in the most unlikely places—the courtyard of the Palazzo Broletto in Brescia, for instance, and without any well-defined reason: "It is a spot where one *catches happiness* just as in other places one catches the plague." This same joyous mood pervades Giono when he stands for twenty minutes in front of the café Pedrocchi in Padua where his beloved Stendhal used to sit on the terrace, or when in Florence he walks along the quays of the Arno where Machiavelli must once have trod.

IV Voyage en Italie

A review of Giono's *Voyage en Italie* (1954) in the London *Times Literary Supplement* asserts that Giono's gifts as a novelist, "his feeling for the countryside, his understanding of the large part the forces of nature play in human affairs, his sensitive perception and description of atmosphere . . . admirably equip him to write a travel book." [4] It is true that Giono manages to convey in a few vivid sentences the essential differences among Italian cities even when he has seen them for only a few hours after dark, and we have also occasional flashes of picturesque landscape, particularly on the drive through the Apennines from Bologna to Florence. Yet Giono warns us frankly that he is not a tourist: "I want to relate only feelings. Globetrotters and men of wit have said all there is to say about the rest." Conscious of the fact that his travel notes "are singularly lacking in descriptions à la Chateaubriand," Giono admits that, though once he too would have taken pleasure in orchestrating the theme of "Emilia by twilight," now he would give all the phrases of nature painting for a few true words on the character of Emilians themselves.

While French and English critics have enthusiastically lauded *Voyage en Italie*, it is easy to understand the reserve of Italian critics, such as Marcello Spaziani, who, in the article already quoted à propos of Giono's *Machiavelli*, considers a love for paradoxes to be inherent in Giono's personality. As a consequence, Spaziani finds the *Voyage* amusing but entirely too flippant and subjective. Indeed, Giono's jovial irreverence for traditional values recalls that of Mark Twain in *Innocents Abroad* and in *Travels Abroad*. One may find a parallel, for instance, between Giono's dismissal of that "monster" the Milan Duomo as not worth "un pet de lapin" because the excessive richness of its two thousand statues is too far away for visibility and the American humorist's ironic eulogy of the harmony of Saint Mark's in Venice, a harmony in which there is not one single detail of beauty to mar its complete ugliness. Mark Twain, disillusioned with his ride on a glacier during which the scenery changed so little after several hours, would also have chuckled merrily at the many humorous misadventures in Giono's *Voyage,* among them the strange propensity of Antoine (Giono's friend and driver) to have his intuition for directions always lead him on the wrong route. Risible also is Giono's discomfiture after having announced solemnly, after a glance at his guidebook, that the fires they were passing were "emanations of hydrogen and protocarbonate giving the impression that one is seeing a conflagration" when he learns on closer approach that they were ordinary bonfires of twigs and branches.

In spite of the many revealing insights into Italian character afforded by the *Voyage,* its greatest charm, as Maurice Pons has pointed out, is "the discovery of a marvelous personage, very much alive, Jean Giono himself, who discloses to us the secret of his happiness. Always natural, spontaneous, sparkling, Giono amazes us all by himself and tells us in truth more about himself than his travels." [5] Surely there has never been a more subjective travelogue. "I have tried to describe the world," says the author, "not as it is but as it is when I add myself to it, which, obviously, does not simplify it." The student of art will learn little here, for Giono confesses frankly: "I don't know how to discuss painting; it is an art that I came to understand late in life (assuming that I understand it even now)." At the same time he suggests puckishly that most people are like him in this respect—but they are unwilling to admit it. Giono avows his lack of interest in political matters; but, though he is "far from believing in the good savage or the good no matter who," his genial indulgence allows him to find everywhere in the common man traits of generosity and compassion that are not incompatible with egotism and ambition.

If we miss in these pages a description of the Roman arena in Verona or of the Grand Canal in Venice, let us not complain. In their place we may watch in consternation with Giono the horrific and stupendous machine which in its earth-shaking eruption produces various flavors of coffee. A final compensation is the priceless recipe which the author gives us for successful *pesca frita!*

V *Giono and His Neighbors*

On his return from Italy, Giono joined a hundred journalists to report the twelve-day trial at Digne that resulted in the death sentence for Gaston Dominici, an elderly peasant accused of assassinating three English tourists—father, mother and daughter—as they slept in the open air after attending a "bull fight." Giono's shrewd analysis of the trial and the witnesses, similar to many of his own characters, formed the material for four articles in *Arts*, a magazine, before being published in 1955 in booklet form. Without reaching a definite conclusion, Giono pointed out many weaknesses and inconsistencies in the case for the prosecution which left him gravely disturbed by the final verdict.

The reader will recall that the first volume of the *Hussard* cycle, chronologically though not in time of composition, was the novel *L'Ecossais*. The circumstances surrounding the writing of this book I learned from Giono himself. In 1955 Giono proposed to the Manosque Rotary Club, of which he was a member, a plan to raise money for the elderly inhabitants who were in want. "We used to meet for supper every Tuesday" Giono related, "merely to exchange stories. I didn't think that was fulfilling the purpose of Rotary. Everybody is doing something for the young; no one pays any attention to the old." Giono then offered to write a book, *L'Ecossais*, to be published in a de luxe edition of eighteen hundred copies by the Manosque printer and sold for fifteen hundred francs by the members of the club. The result was a profit of three million francs, enough "to provide for them wood in winter, a chicken in the pot every Sunday, a little wine and other comforts for three years." This incident may help to explain Giono's widespread popularity among the natives of his little town.

VI *The Cinema*

In 1956 Giono was engaged by Electricité de France to undertake a sociological study of the effect produced by the great new dam in the Durance valley on the inhabitants of the region, forced to leave their homes as the water rose to inundate their former villages and farms. An interesting by-product of this study was Giono's technicolor film *L'Eau vive,* which in 1960 was having a successful run in London. The dialogue is realistic and captivating in itself, particularly for its depiction of the hardfisted, cantankerous peasants whose avarice and jealousy Giono knows so well. Even more fascinating, however, is the magnificent setting of river and mountainside, including the highly scenic new lake near Gap which does not yet appear on most maps but which seems destined to rival lakes Annecy and Bourget as tourist attractions.

Encouraged by this venture, Giono decided in the spring of 1960 not only to write the scenario for the film *Crésus,* but also to share its direction—with Claude Pinoteau as technical assistant—and its financial sponsorship—with its principal actor, the great French comic star Fernandel. The story was suggested by an actual incident which occurred during World War II when the retreating Germans dropped bundles of counterfeit paper money in order to throw the French economy into confusion.

In the film Jules (an ignorant shepherd played by Fernandel) finds in an unexploded bomb a huge bundle of five thousand franc notes, thinks himself a multimillionaire, and begins to spend with lavish hand. Discouraged, however, by his inability to make any inroads on this colossal package—too enormous for the coffers of the little banks in Forcalquier—Jules first invites the denizens of his village to a truly bacchanalian feast, then distributes huge quantities of paper money among the various homes. Ironically enough, instead of making every one happy as he had expected, he is astonished to find that his generosity has created suspicion of his motives and mutual antagonisms among the populace. When the police arrive at last to confiscate all this spurious wealth, it is with a sigh of relief that Jules discards his store-bought finery in favor of his comfortable old jeans before offering his hand to the one woman who, untouched by his sudden prosperity, had refused to join in the hue and cry against him. As a feature of the première in Paris in the autumn of 1960 each member of the audience was presented with a counterfeit five thousand franc note on which the likeness of François Premier had been replaced with the grotesque features of Fernandel.

In his choice of the rustic plateau of Contadour as locale for this production Giono gives evidence of nostalgia for his youth, for this was once the site of his back-to-nature crusade in the 1930's.

When one tries to drive over the ruts and sharp stones of this desert tableland, from which it seems that half of France must be visible, one marvels at the vitality of Fernandel who arrived on location in a cloud of dust every morning after the seventy- or eighty-mile drive in his heavy Cadillac from Marseilles.

In 1961 *Crésus* was published in a limited de luxe edition in the form of its original "script for movie director." It will be of particular value to those interested in cinema technique, and it possesses the additional attraction of drawings by Lucien Jacques, doubtless the last work completed before his death.

In an interview with Madeleine Chapsal, Giono recently discussed some of the difficulties he finds in this new medium. The chief difference between the novel and the cinema is a technical one which involves the participation of a large group of people and the consequent expense. As Giono whimsically summarizes: "With the pen, if I want an army, a hundred thousand corpses, I have them, I need only imagine them. With the cinema it's quite different, they have to be really procured, that costs money, that takes time." [6] To one who knows Giono only as the solitary figure, who is contemptuous of modern gadgets and who writes with the cloistered perseverance of a Benedictine monk in his library, it is difficult to think of him in charge of fifty men in the hurly-burly of a movie production. It is not surprising therefore to hear him say that the joys of a motion picture director are inferior to those involved in the work of a writer, and that he does not expect to continue his efforts in the cinema. But we cannot be sure. If the stage with its concentration on characterization and its limited scope for lyric description seems hardly the most appropriate vehicle for Giono's special genius, the cinema, on the other hand, with its opportunity for picturesque background and unlimited adventures cannot fail to attract Giono's mobile and versatile nature—one ever ready to explore new paths, overflowing with vitality and creative energy at the age of seventy-one. [7]

VII *Reactions to Our Era*

In the seclusion of his "light house" Giono is perhaps as unconcerned with politics or the "cold war" as any one living today. In an interview with Guy Bechtel he expressed equal indifference to Russian sputniks and to American exploration in the field of space: "Nothing modern touches me profoundly. Take the H bomb for instance. If it falls on me, so much the worse. I prefer not to think of it in advance, it would be a waste of time. To solve the only important problem in life—the pursuit of happiness—an artificial satellite is of little aid." [8] A distant echo of Francesc Odripano's comment on the first flight of the Wright brothers is audible in Giono's comment that man was given senses, intelligence, and curiosity to make his happiness; and "if one goes to the moon, it will be decidedly *not* to use our senses. In the night, in the silence, man will hardly need them. He will be diminished, hence less happy."

After viewing the "monsters" of contemporary architecture at the Brussels Exposition, Giono insists that he sees no improvement since the building of the Gallo-Roman houses still to be found in his region. Not that he is the enemy of progress, if it is useful. Thus he adores his electric phonograph because it brings him Mozart. On the other hand, he despises the typewriter and still more the dictaphone. Once, when he had dictated a whole book into this machine, the result was so pitiable that he was obliged to recommence from the beginning, using one or the other of the fifty quill pens to be seen on his table. Indeed, this preference for the pen may have had an amusing and decisive influence on his work. Once a few years ago, when he was suffering from terrible arthritis in his wrist, he nevertheless forced himself to continue writing with his swollen hand: "How long the adjectives were, how heavy the adverbs!" "Did you omit them?" "Yes, almost all, and it was just as well. They caused me too much pain. But this suffering finally amused me and at the end I believe that this text, more precise, more simple, was a good one." Some day Giono, with his fondness for paradoxes, may smile if this statement should be seized as a clue by the writer of a doctoral dissertation seeking to explain the change so visible in Giono's mature style.

In the spring of 1960 there appeared in most French newspapers a violent declaration of Giono's intention to abandon his residence in Manosque because his beloved town had been ruined by the encroachments of modern civilization. The immediate cause for this outburst seems to have been the employment of bulldozers to raze several blocks of houses full of medieval charm but unsanitary and perhaps even dangerous because of crumbling walls. The increasing industrialization of the Durance valley and particularly the new atomic installations just below Manosque seem destined to increase the population of the city four or five fold, and already huge new apartment houses have begun to invade the peaceful slopes of Giono's Mont d'Or.

When asked where he intended to move, Giono mentioned Aix-en-Provence. He has many ties with this happy, carefree city of which the Cours Mirabeau, lined by eighteenth-century houses and by sycamores forming with their foliage a canopy over the moss-covered fountains, has been termed the most beautiful avenue in France. He is a frequent visitor to the Festival which every July offers Mozart's operas in the courtyard of the Archbishop's Palace. On the terrace of the famous Café des Deux Garçons might have been seen sipping fruit juices, black coffee or the insiduously disarming *pastis* not only the young bloods of the city but tourists from Holland or Germany here for the Festival, music critics from Paris, and at times such notables as Cocteau from Nice, Buffet the painter, or even Giono himself. The venerable cathedral and the medieval bell tower with its ancient clock dominate the narrow streets of the old city. Perhaps Giono would be contented here, yet even Aix is beginning to lose some of its atmosphere as it makes room for the industrial prosperity which is rudely awakening Provence from the lethargy of past centuries. It may be that Giono has had second thoughts, for several years have passed since he uttered his threat—and he still lives midst his rosebushes on the Mount of Gold. He is still "the man from Manosque," though every summer he spends a month on his newly acquired estate on Mallorca near Palma.

CHAPTER 18

Conclusion

I *Successive Images*

IN the Preface to the recent de luxe edition of his first publication, *Accompagnés de la flûte*, Giono asserts: "The portrait of the artist by himself which I was to paint later in almost fifty novels was already perfected here." It is true that few authors have revealed themselves more frankly in their works, but the variety of his production is so rich that the impression of the author's personality revealed is exceedingly complex and even paradoxical.

The first image projected by Giono's writings in the early 1930's was that of a naïve, self-tutored rustic, emerging from his provincial hibernation on his infrequent visits to the metropolis to amaze the sophisticated Parisians with his sheepskin coat and his dour suspicion of the artificiality he found in contemporary civilization. Our next vision was that of the sage of Contadour, a nature prophet, revered with almost mystic devotion by the starry-eyed young idealists who came as pilgrims from the far corners of Europe to his shrine. By a natural enough transition this image was soon enlarged and transformed into that of the social revolutionary, insistent that the menace of war hanging like a black cloud over Europe, together with the frustrations and spiritual emptiness of industrialized society, could only be exorcised by a return to the life of the peasant and artisan. In his anarchistic diatribes against parties and governments Giono presaged "the angry young men" of the England of the 1950's.

These characteristics do not represent the Giono of today who has abandoned the modest Hotel du Dragon for a more elegant hostelry when he comes to Paris to join his nine colleagues at the annual luncheon chez Drouant to choose the recipient of the Prix Goncourt. Gone today is his facile if generous optimism, but he has not become bitter and hard. Disillusioned by the rejection of his message, Giono is now the keen observer rather than the reformer of men. "I adore men, I love them very much," Giono confided recently to an interviewer; but he quickly added: "I have no confidence in humanity. Oh, for lots of things I have confidence. I am confident that they will perpetuate many abominable things. . . . But I have no confidence in the perfectability of the human race." [1] Giono feels, for instance, that wars will continue to recur because of man's insatiable desire for violent action.

The paradoxes inherent in Giono's protean character bring despair to the critic seeking to summarize him with a brief generalization. One of his biographers, Romée de Villeneuve, has entitled his study *Giono ce solitaire,* and it has become customary to stress the solitude in which Giono lives and works—a solitude exemplified also by many of the heroes of his books. Giono does indeed enjoy the pleasures of his rose garden, of his isolated "light house" with its shelves of well-thumbed books, of his pipes and little Brazilian cigars, of his lonely walks through his familiar countryside. Yet in many ways this patient, hard-working anchorite is the most gregarious of men; devoted to family and associates, he has a warm welcome for friends; he is a familiar figure among the humble citizens of Manosque and is even a participant in the weekly banquets of Rotary!

Restricted by his obligations as breadwinner for numerous dependents to spending most of his youth and maturity in the narrow perimeter of Provence and the Alps, Giono is now an indefatigable traveler whose peregrinations have extended to Scotland, Italy, and other countries of Europe. Still as ardent a pacifist as ever, Giono is yet a true descendant of his swaggering grandfather in his fascination for military pomp and glory, as shown in his *Bonheur fou* and in his recent treatise on the Battle of Pavia. Professing a disdainful indifference towards the articles of hostile critics, Giono nevertheless shows himself well acquainted with every essay or monograph concerning his work. Guarding jealously his independence and imbued with absolute confidence in his own development, Giono on the other hand is capable of surprising humility in agreeing with the suggestions of others.

There are, however, some qualities in Giono which, though they may have been overshadowed at times, have remained constant from the very beginning of his career. The reader will recall Lucien Jacques' comment that in the Odysseus of *Naissance de l'Odyssée* Giono has given a rather unflattering portrait of himself. Here we see, perhaps, Giono's besetting sin, which may be a key, however, to his success as a novelist: his temptation to transform the humble truth into a shining, glittering amalgam of distortion, made much more amusing and attractive than unvarnished reality. For this reason, an interviewer must be somewhat on his guard with Giono, and will at times be puzzled by conflicting interpretations of the same incident. Perhaps in this respect Giono is a typical representative of méridional verve and *démesure;* carried away by his vibrant vitality, Giono makes promises which are undoubtedly sincere but which he completely forgets a short time later. One has the impression that, in this magic world which Giono is constantly superimposing on reality, the magician has often bewitched himself as well as his listener.

In other respects, Giono has also remained a thoroughly human character. The wealth showered on him by his literary success has made no change in his frugal existence, and apparently he is completely indifferent to the gadgets and luxuries he could now afford. His idea of a pleasant outing is still to find some modest inn by the river bank which can tempt the palate with a freshly caught fish or other local delicacy. The flashes of ironic humor first apparent in *Naissance de l'Odyssée* but so long obscured by his sensuous absorption in nature, then by the seriousness with which he took his social mission, have now been given free rein as he contemplates with amused indulgence the foibles of mankind. His greatest joy is still in his work, and his absolute serenity amidst a world of H-bombs and space missiles is an almost incredible phenomenon in an age of doubt and suspicion. Who shall say whether this represents egotism or supreme wisdom?

II *A Timid Prophecy*

If we glance from the man himself to his prolific production, a hasty and no doubt incomplete enumeration of the authors to whom he has been compared by the critics of several countries would include such names as Homer, Stendhal, Melville, Victor Hugo, Ramuz, Tolstoi, and such contemporaries as D. H. Lawrence, Camus, and Faulkner. Even if we make due allowance for the exaggeration to which some of his admirers have been carried, it is at least a striking tribute to Giono's versatility that his name could be mentioned with so many of the world's masters. The lush richness of Giono's fertile creativity reminds one indeed of a tropical jungle in which the explorer must first thrust aside the underbrush in order to feast his eyes on the exotic splendor of the foliage and fauna.

In this very profusion, however, lies one of Giono's greatest failings. Was it Voltaire, speaking in old age of his own production, who remarked prophetically, "one does not pass into posterity with so much baggage?" When Gide once inquired of Giono if writing were painful for him, Giono's answer was characteristic: "If I suffered, I wouldn't write. I'm not Job." Indeed, writing at least four pages a day is for Giono an inner compulsion which neither holidays nor the death of a loved one can impede. Like Alexandre Dumas *père* and Michelet, Giono can truly be likened to "a force of nature." Of his enormous production, it is certain that much will prove merely ephemeral; it is unlikely that his dramas, motion picture scenarios, travelogues, propaganda pamphlets, even most of his short stories and sketches, will be long remembered.

What will remain will in all likelihood be only a handful of his novels—but enough to assure him a permanent and distinguished rank among the great novelists of France. Literary prophecy is perhaps the most dangerous and futile of all human temptations, and full of temerity is he who dares to foretell the taste of future generations. Like the poetaster in Molière's *Les Femmes Savantes,* who first castigated the mania of his contemporaries for declaiming their verses in public, then proceeded to pull from his pocket and read the poem he had just written, I will suppress my own personal fondness for *Pour saluer Melville* and *Voyage en Italie,* and venture my nominations for survival among Giono's works. Of Giono's first period this list would include *Jean le bleu,* the short volumes of the *Trilogy of Pan* now available in inexpensive editions for the masses, and especially that beautiful and poetic *Chant du Monde;* of the post-war period the strangely haunting *Un Roi sans divertissement* and *Les Ames fortes,* and certainly *Le Hussard sur le toit.* If any one reading these pages should be alive in the year 2007, it might be interesting for him to decide whether Giono, like Stendhal, has won his wager in regard to *Le Bonheur fou.*

III   *Faults*

Giono's numerous weaknesses as a novelist stem primarily from the characteristics already mentioned: prolixity and proliferation.

In most of them there is great unevenness, resulting in majestic mountain peaks worthy of an anthology that alternate with dreary wasteland and monotonous marshes in which the reader is bogged down. In the earlier period Giono's verbosity keeps him from resting until he has almost smothered the reader with adjectival synonyms and breathless metaphors. On other occasions his quest for naturalness led him into the artifice of elementary dialogue, replete with irregular syntax and repetition. His absorption with natural forces sometimes tended to diminish his human figures until they were scarcely distinguishable from plant or animal creation.

Until he reached the sophistication of his later manner, Giono showed himself to be occasionally a trifle clumsy and awkward in his technique. Commenting on the magnificent epic passage which opens *Le Grand Troupeau,* one critic contended that Giono was rarely able to sustain throughout his novels the lofty tone of their beginning chapters. Actually, the reverse is more often the case. Like Balzac, Giono sometimes has difficulty plunging in *medias res;* and in many novels, such as *Batailles dans la montagne, Les Ames fortes,* and *Le Bonheur fou,* the reader becomes discouraged by the confusion and tedium of the exposition before he reaches the truly dramatic scenes in which the plot unfolds. In all fairness to Giono, however, it should be said that he would be the first to agree with this criticism.

IV *Virtues*

But, if Giono has several faults, they are more than redeemed by virtues which in many cases are merely the obverse of the medal and spring from the same source. Thus his prolixity is only the price he pays for verve and intensity—a richness of the creative imagination which few writers have exceeded. In the most recent and perhaps most authoritative summation of his work, Robert Kanters has pointed out that Giono's production represents a sort of mountain range outside the well-traveled routes of contemporary ideas and fashions: "No one contests that he is among our greatest writers, if they are counted, let us say, on the fingers of both hands. If he has links with other mountain ranges, distant from us in time (Rousseau, Stendhal), these relations come less from affiliation or influence than from an inner affinity." [2] André Malraux would include Giono, along with Montherlant and Bernanos, in his choice for the three best writers of this generation. Paul Morand in his moving tribute to Giono, which forms the Preface to Pugnet's book so often cited here, goes so far as to suggest that Giono would be a worthy recipient for the Nobel Prize in literature.

Giono is first of all a great poet in prose. It is now generally recognized that, like Chateaubriand in the preceding century, he has brought a new freshness, warmth, and color to the French language. "I am a sensualist," Jean le bleu had said of himself; and a sensualist Giono has remained though he now disciplines and tempers his naïve *épanchements*. Uniquely open to the physical universe, he has given man a new vision of the reality about him, and expressed it with a wealth of imagery and symbol. Closely akin to this quality in Giono is his ability to transport us into a world of fantasy and mystery which yet seems entirely credible and real.

If Giono has succeeded in readapting to our blasé, sophisticated society the long-forgotten tradition of the primitive epic, he has also shown himself a precursor and initiator in the technique of the modern novel. Better than any other contemporary French novelist, perhaps, he has practiced the method of Faulkner and the American novel in allowing the reader to participate more fully in the explanation of events and characters overlapping in time as they are related in the first person by one or more humble narrators. In his experimentation with new techniques of ellipsis and discontinuity in the *Chroniques*, including *Le Bonheur fou*, and presumably in the long-awaited *Pauline*, Giono, unlike Mauriac and many other writers, gives evidence of creative renewal and vitality which may well hold further surprises for us.

In one respect, however, Giono is far removed from contemporary practice. Recent tendencies in the novel seem to subordinate the story itself to the "stream of consciousness" technique until one critic has complained that "the history of fiction is simply the history of the decay of the plot." Other than his poetic spontaneity, the most persistent quality in Giono as a novelist has been his marvelous capacity for telling a story that holds the reader breathless until the end. It was this power that Giono used to calm the jittery fears of his comrades in the front lines, or to while away the tedium of his fellow prisoners in the courtyard of Fort Saint-Nicolas. Snobbish intellectuals have decried this quality in Giono by comparing him to Dumas *père* or to Eugène Sue. It remains to be seen, however, whether the pendulum may not swing back once more, for already there are many who find lacking in warmth and interest the dissections of soul states and the enumeration of objects in the contemporary novel.

And finally, the last paradox we shall mention in regard to this paradoxical writer, Giono the regionalist is at the same time a universal writer. Once more the close parallel with Faulkner comes to mind. Almost all the latter's characters live and move and have their being in the tiny rural county of Yoknapatawpha in his native Mississippi, and he would seem to be the epitome of the regionalist writer. So broadly human, however, are these creations of Faulkner, so common to all mankind are their tragic fates that Faulkner, winner of the Nobel Prize for literature, is now as widely read in France and Europe as in his own country. Similarly Giono's novels, except for Angélo's exploits in Italy, are all concentrated in the comparatively wild and primitive valleys and plateaux of upper Provence and Dauphiné. But, though we recognize the scenery and even the faces of his characters, Giono is far more than a regional novelist. His themes are universal and timeless—the struggle of man for survival against the great forces of nature; the elemental and eternal instincts of love and friendship, ambition and revenge.

Contrary to the despair and frustration of many Existentialists with their conviction of the absurdity of human life, the general impression emanating from Giono's pages—even from those describing cruelty and pestilence—is one of animation and action rather than of spineless submission to fate. Malraux was justified in saying that Giono, Montherlant, Bernanos, and Malraux himself "are bound to what one may call the heroic tradition of France, its Cornelian tradition." "Professor of energy," as Giono has been called in the words he used in defining Machiavelli, and "professor of hope," as he himself wished the artist to be, Giono as a novelist makes an appeal to critics and general public alike.

Notes and References

Chapter One

1. Romée de Villeneuve, *Jean Giono, ce solitaire* (Avignon, 1955), p. 183. Hereafter referred to as Villeneuve.

Chapter Two

1. Henri Peyre, *The Contemporary French Novel* (New York, 1955), p. 134. Hereafter referred to as Peyre.

Chapter Three

1. Claudine Chonez, *Giono peint par lui-même* (Paris, 1956), p. 35. Hereafter referred to as Chonez.
2. Henri Perruchot, "Interview avec Jean Giono," *Réalité* (Paris), LXXXI (Oct., 1952), 79–83.
3. Jacques Pugnet, *Jean Giono* (Paris, 1955), p. 28. Hereafter referred to as Pugnet.
4. Christian Michelfelder, *Jean Giono et les religions de la terre* (Paris, 1938), p. 52. Hereafter referred to as Michelfelder.

Chapter Four

1. André Rousseaux, *Littérature du XXième siècle I* (Paris, 1938), p. 195.
2. Pierre Brodin, *Présences contemporaines* (Paris, 1955), p. 125.
3. André Rousseaux, *Ames et visages du XXième siècle* (Paris, 1932), p. 193.

Chapter Five

1. André Gide, *Autumn Leaves* (New York, 1950), p. 249.

Chapter Six

1. Robert Brasillach, "Batailles dans la montagne," *Action Française* (Paris, Oct. 7, 1937).
2. Louis de Mondadon, "Le Grand Troupeau," *Etudes* (Paris, July 5, 1932).

[179]

3. Henry Miller, *The Books in My Life* (London, 1952), pp. 100–120.

4. Katherine Clarke, *Le Lyrisme dans l'oeuvre de Jean Giono* (thesis, University of Grenoble, 1938), p. 83.

Chapter Seven

1. Henri Malherbe, "Lanceurs de graines," *Revue des Vivants* (Paris, Dec., 1932).

Chapter Eight

1. Firmin Roz, *Revue Politique et Littéraire* (Paris, June 17, 1933).

2. Marcel Arland, "Le Chant du monde," *Nouvelle Revue Française* (Paris, Sept. 1, 1953), pp. 495–505.

3. François Varillon, *Etudes* (Paris, June 2, 1937).

4. Henri Fluchère, "Le Chant du monde," *Cahiers du Sud* (Marseilles, July, 1935), pp. 588–91.

5. Robert Brasillach, "Le Cas Giono," *Les Quatre Jeudis* (Paris, 1951), pp. 312–24.

6. Firmin Roz, "La Manière de M. Jean Giono," *Revue Politique et Littéraire* (Paris, Oct. 16, 1937).

7. Henri Pourrat, "La Pensée Magique de Jean Giono," *Nouvelle Revue Française* (Oct., 1938), pp. 646–58.

8. Henri Bidou, *Feuilleton du Journal des Débats* (Nov. 2, 1937).

9. Jacques Madaule, "Jean Giono," *Reconnaissances II* (Paris, 1943), p. 151.

10. Robert Brasillach, "Batailles dans la montagne," *Action Française* (Paris, Oct. 7, 1937).

11. Christian Michelfelder, *Cahiers du Sud* (Marseilles, Feb. 1938), pp. 144–7.

Chapter Nine

1. Edmond Epardaud, "Une Journée à Manosque avec Jean Giono," *Les Nouvelles Littéraires* (March 13, 1937).

2. Fernand Vial, "Jean Giono at the Académie Goncourt," *The American Society Legion of Honor Magazine* (Spring, 1955), pp. 9–25.

3. Ernst Eric Noth, "A Manosque chez Jean Giono," *Les Nouvelles Littéraires* (Paris, Jan., 1938).

Chapter Ten

1. André Thérive, *Feuilleton du Temps* (Paris, Nov. 24, 1938).

2. *Revue Hebdomadaire* (Paris, Aug. 21–28, 1937).

3. François Varillon, *Etudes* (Paris, Oct. 30, 1938).

4. Robert Kemp, *Le Temps* (Paris, Oct. 30, 1938).

Notes and References

5. Max Brunher, *Atelier* (Paris, May 10, 1939).
6. José Vincent, *La Croix* (Paris, Jan. 16, 1939).
7. Jacques Madaule, "Jean Giono," *Reconnaissances II* (Paris, 1943), pp. 151 ff.
8. Robert Brasillach, "Le Cas Giono," *Les Quatre Jeudis* (Paris, 1951), pp. 312–24.

Chapter Thirteen

1. Pierre Lhoste, "Promenade avec Jean Giono," *Paris Midi* (Jan. 21, 1943).
2. Albert Camus, "Ne Jugez Pas," *Combat* (Paris, Dec. 30, 1944).
3. Jean Paulhan, *Carrefour* (Paris, July 23, 1947).
4. André Gide, "Feuilles d'Automne," No. 6 of *La Table Ronde* (Paris, June 6, 1948); American edition, *Autumn Leaves* (New York, 1950), p. 249.
5. Tristan Tzara, "Un Romancier de la Lâcheté," *Lettres Françaises* (Paris, Oct. 6, 1944).

Chapter Fourteen

1. Christian Millau, "Rencontre avec Jean Giono, académicien sans uniforme," *Carrefour* (Paris, Jan. 12, 1955), p. 9.

Chapter Fifteen

1. Marcel Arland, "Un Nouveau Giono," *Lettres de France* (Paris, 1951), pp. 158–65.
2. Maurice Nadeau, "Un Nouveau Giono," *Mercure de France* (Paris, April 1, 1950), pp. 693–7.
3. Pierre Robert, *Jean Giono et les Techniques du Roman* (Berkeley and Los Angeles, 1961), p. 27.
4. Jean Onimus, "L'Expression du temps dans le Roman," *Revue de Littérature Comparée* (Paris, 1954), p. 314.
5. Robert Kanters, "Jean Giono avant et après le déluge," *Le Figaro Littéraire* (Paris, June 3, 1961), p. 2.
6. René Lalou, "Le Moulin de Pologne," *Les Annales-Conférencia* (Paris, April, 1953), pp. 15–19.
7. Giacomo Antonini, "Jean Giono e il Castigo di Dio," *La Fiera Letteraria* (Rome, June 21, 1953), p. 4.
8. André Rousseaux, *Le Figaro Littéraire* (Paris, March 1, 1953).

Chapter Sixteen

1. Marcel Arland, "A la Hussarde," *Nouvelle Revue Française* (Paris, Oct., 1953), pp. 687–96.
2. Walter Orlando, "La Voie Libre," *La Table Ronde* (Paris, Jan., 1952), pp. 143–5.

3. Dominique Aury, "Un Chef d'oeuvre de Giono," *Arts* (Paris, Jan. 11, 1952), p. 3.

4. "Jean Giono or Characters in Control of an Author," *Times Literary Supplement* (London, May 27, 1955), p. 14.

5. Mario Maurin, "Le Bonheur fou," *Les Lettres Nouvelles*, 52 (Paris, Sept., 1957), 304–5.

6. André Rousseaux, "Jean Giono, seconde manière," *Le Figaro Littéraire* (Paris, May 7, 1953), p. 2.

7. Maurice Thiébaut, "Les Deux Giono," *Revue de Paris* (June, 1957), pp. 143–51.

8. Gaëtan Picon, "Le Bonheur fou," *Mercure de France, MCXXIX* (Paris, Sept., 1957), pp. 122–6.

9. Mario Maurin, *op. cit.*

10. Gennie Luccioni, "Jean Giono: Le Bonheur fou," *Esprit* (Paris, Sept., 1957), pp. 292–7.

11. Jean Larnac, *La Pensée*, 25 (Paris, July-Aug., 1949), pp. 107–116.

12. Louis Chaigne, *Vie et oeuvres d'écrivains* (Paris, 1956), pp. 1965–78.

Chapter Seventeen

1. Claudine Chonez, "Une Journée de Giono à Manosque," *Le Figaro Littéraire* (Paris, Dec. 11, 1954), p. 5.

2. Christian Millau, "Rencontre avec J. Giono, académicien sans uniforme," *Carrefour* (Paris, Jan. 12, 1955), p. 9.

3. Marcello Spaziani, "Jean Giono in Italia," *Fiera Letteraria* (Rome, April 4, 1954), pp. 1–2.

4. "Individual Traveler: Jean Giono," *Times Literary Supplement* (London, Aug. 13, 1954), p. 515.

5. Maurice Pons, "Leçon de bonheur en voyage," *La Table Ronde* (Paris, June, 1954), pp. 152–6.

6. Madeleine Chapsal, "Un Homme heureux" (interview), *L'Express* (Paris, March 21, 1960), pp. 33–7.

7. Since this was written, Giono's novel *Un Roi sans divertissement* has been filmed.

8. Guy Bechtel, *Carrefour* (interview) (Paris, May 14, 1958), pp. 7, 9.

Chapter Eighteen

1. Madeleine Chapsal, "Un Homme heureux," *L'Express* (Paris, March 21, 1960), pp. 33–7.

2. Robert Kanters, "Jean Giono, avant et après le déluge," *Le Figaro Littéraire* (Paris, June 3, 1961), p. 2.

Selected Bibliography

I. *Primary Sources*   (*Novels marked with asterisk*)

Accompagnés de la flûte. Gréoux: Les Cahiers de l'Artisan, 1924.

* *Colline*. Paris: Grasset, 1929. *Hill of Destiny*. Tr. by Jacques Le Clerq. New York: Brentano, (1929)

* *Un de Baumugnes*. Paris: Grasset, 1929. *Lovers Are Never Losers*. Tr. by Jacques Le Clerq. London: Jarrolds, 1932.

Présentation de Pan. Paris: Grasset, 1930.

* *Regain*. Paris: Grasset, 1930. *Harvest*. Tr. by Henri Fluchère and Geoffrey Meyers. London and Toronto: Wm. Heinemann, 1939.

* *Naissance de l'Odyssée*. Marseilles: Kra., 1930; Paris: Grasset, 1938.

Manosque des plateaux. Paris: Emile Paul, 1930.

* *Le Grand Troupeau*. Paris: *Nouvelle Revue Française*, 1931.

* *Solitude de la pitié*, Paris: *Nouvelle Revue Française*, 1931.

* *Jean le bleu*. Paris: Grasset, 1932. *Blue Boy*. Tr. by Katherine Clarke. New York: Viking, 1949; London: Routledge and Kegan, Paul, 1949.

* *Le Serpent d'étoiles*. Paris: Grasset, 1933.

* *Le Chant du monde*. Paris: *Nouvelle Revue Française*, 1934. *The Song of the World*. Tr. by Henri Fluchère and Geoffrey Meyers. New York: Viking, 1938; London and Toronto: Wm. Heinemann, 1938.

* *Que ma joie demeure*. Paris: Grasset, 1935. *Joy of Man's Desiring*. Tr. by Katherine Clarke. New York: Viking, 1949; London: Routledge and Kegan Paul, 1949.

Les Vraies Richesses. Paris: Grasset, 1936.

* *Batailles dans la montagne*. Paris: *Nouvelle Revue Française*, 1937.

Refus d'obéissance. Paris: *Nouvelle Revue Française*, 1937.

La Provence. (Album des guides bleus). Paris: Hachette, 1954.

* *L'Ecossais*. Manosque: Rico et Auphan, 1955.

Le Poids du ciel. Paris: *Nouvelle Revue Française*, 1938.

Lettre aux paysans sur la pauvreté et la paix. Paris: Grasset, 1938.

Précisions. Paris: Grasset, 1939.

Triomphe de la vie. Paris: Grasset, 1942.

Moby Dick. Tr. by Jean Giono, Lucien Jacques, and Joan Smith. Paris: Gallimard, 1943.

* *Pour saluer Melville.* Paris: *Nouvelle Revue Française,* 1943.

Théâtre. Le Bout de la Route, Lanceurs de graines, La Femme du boulanger. Paris: *Nouvelle Revue Française,* 1943.

L'Eau vive. Paris: *Nouvelle Revue Française,* 1944.

Voyage en calèche. Monaco: Editions du Rocher, 1946.

Virgile. Paris: Corrêa, 1947.

* *Un Roi sans divertissement.* Paris: Le Table Ronde. *Nouvelle Revue Française,* 1947.

* *Noé.* Paris: La Table Ronde, 1947; Gallimard, 1961.

* *Mort d'un personnage.* Paris: Grasset, 1949.

* *Les Ames fortes.* Paris: *Nouvelle Revue Française,* 1949.

* *Les Grands Chemins.* Paris: *Nouvelle Revue Française,* 1951.

* *Le Hussard sur le toit.* Paris: *Nouvelle Revue Française,* 1951. *The Hussar on the Roof.* Tr. by Jonathan Griffen. London: The Museum Press, 1954. *The Horseman on the Roof.* New York: Alfred A. Knopf, 1954.

Préface aux Oeuvres complètes de Machiavel. Paris: *Nouvelle Revue Française,* 1951.

* *Le Moulin de Pologne.* Paris: *Nouvelle Revue Française,* 1952. *The Malediction.* Tr. by Peter de Mendelssohn. London: Museum Press, 1955; New York: Criterion Books, 1955.

Voyage en Italie. Paris: *Nouvelle Revue Française,* 1953.

Notes sur l'affaire Dominici. Paris: Gallimard, 1955.

* *Le Bonheur fou.* Paris: Gallimard, *Nouvelle Revue Française,* 1957. *The Straw Man.* Tr. by Phyllis Johnson. New York: Alfred A. Knopf, 1959.

* *Angélo.* Paris: Gallimard, *Nouvelle Revue Française,* 1958.

Domitien, suivi de Joseph à Dothan. Paris: *Nouvelle Revue Française,* Gallimard, 1959.

Accompagnés de la flûte, avec Introduction et lettres à Lucien Jacques. Manosque: Rico et Auphan, 1960.

Crésus (Livre de conduite de metteur en scène). Manosque: Rico et Auphan, 1961.

Le Désastre de Pavie. Paris: Gallimard, 1963.

Giono—Selections. Ed. by Maxwell A. Smith. Boston: D. C. Heath and Co., 1965.

* *Deux Cavaliers de l'orage.* Paris: Gallimard, 1965.

II. Secondary Sources

ANONYMOUS. "Jean Giono or Characters in Control of an Author," *The (London) Times Literary Supplement* (May 27, 1955), p. 14. Probably the best article in English on Giono's post-war novels and his place in the contemporary novel.

Selected Bibliography

ARLAND, MARCEL. *Lettres de France*. Paris: Albin Michel, 1951. Excellent discussion of "the new Giono," particularly as revealed in *Les Ames fortes*.

————. *La Grace d'écrire*. Paris: Gallimard, 1955. Perhaps the best appreciation in French of Giono's two masterpieces, *Le Chant du monde* and *Le Hussard sur le toit*. The same articles may also be found in the *Nouvelle Revue Française* (Sept., 1953), pp. 495–505; (Oct. 1953), pp. 687–96.

BOISDEFFRE, PIERRE DE. *Giono*. Paris: Gallimard, 1965. Excellent for the student of Giono. Chronology, discussion of his work, summaries of his books with excerpts from each, appreciation by critics.

BRASILLACH, ROBERT. "Le Cas Giono," *Les Quatre Jeudis*. Paris: Balzac, 1951. A somewhat unfavorable critic of Giono's early epic novels; Brasillach is, however, stimulating and witty.

BRÉE, GERMAINE AND GUITON, MARGARET. *The French Novel from Gide to Camus*. New York: Harcourt Brace and World, 1962. In my opinion does scant justice to Giono, particularly to his later work.

CHONEZ, CLAUDINE. *Giono par lui-même*. Paris: Editions du Seuil, Collection, Ecrivains de Toujours, 1956. Particularly valuable for its many illustrations and for its well-chosen excerpts which give an idea of Giono's style in various works.

CLARKE, KATHERINE A. *Le Lyrisme dans l'œuvre de Jean Giono*. Grenoble: *thèse*, Uni. de Grenoble, 1938. One of the first studies of Giono's earlier lyric period and still one of the best. Miss Clarke had the advantage of frequent discussions with Giono himself.

————. "Pour saluer Melville. Jean Giono's Prison Book." *The French Review XXXV* (April 1962), 478–83. Of special interest for influence of Melville on Giono.

————. "An Interview with Jean Giono." *The French Review XXXIII* (Oct., 1959), 3–10. Because this was a tape recording, this interview gives an intimate picture of Giono's attitude towards his work, and particularly his solitary heroes.

FLUCHÈRE, HENRI. "Reflexions sur Jean Giono," *Cahiers du Sud*, 19 (1932), 144–9. The writer, formerly a professor of English at the university of Aix-en-Provence, knew Giono personally and translated two of his books.

————. "Le Chant du monde," *Cahiers du Sud* (July, 1935), pp. 588–91. Excellent appreciation by the translator of this novel into English.

GILMAN, WAYNE C., JR. "The General Neologisms of Jean Giono."

The French Review, XXXIII (April, 1960), 469–75. Scholarly article of special interest to students of Giono's style.

KANTERS, ROBERT. "Jean Giono, avant et après le déluge." *Le Figaro Littéraire* (June 3, 1961), p. 2. Begun as a review of Giono's re-printing of *Noé*, this perceptive article by one of the leading French critics of today attempts to assess the work of Giono and his rank in the French novel.

MICHELFELDER, CHRISTIAN. *Jean Giono et les religions de la terre.* Paris: Gallimard, 1938. Covers only the first part of Giono's work and is somewhat unbalanced by the critic's insistence on relating everything to Greek mythology, but still a useful book.

MILLER, HENRY. *The Books in My Life.* London: Peter Owen; New York: New Directions, 1952. This essay is an impassioned eulogy rather than a critical analysis.

NADEAU, MAURICE. "Un Nouveau Giono," *Littérature Présente*. Paris: Corrêa. 1952, pp. 135–141. Interesting comparison of Giono's new manner in the *Chroniques* to that of Greek tragedy. Same essay in *Mercure de France* (April 1, 1950), pp. 693–7.

PEYRE, HENRI. *The Contemporary French Novel.* New York: Oxford University Press, 1955. By far the best analysis of Giono's work which has yet appeared in English, though perhaps it does not quite do justice to Giono's later works, other than *Le Hussard sur le toit*.

PICON, GAËTAN. "Le Bonhêur fou," *Mercure de France*, MCXXIX (Sept., 1957), 122–6. By far the best article on this novel, and very original in its treatment of Giono's modernistic technique.

POMERAI, ODILE DE ."An Unknown Giono". *The French Review* XXXIX, (Oct. 1965) pp. 78–84. Good account of plot and symbolism of Giono's *Deux Cavaliers de l'orage*, recently published in book form.

PUGNET, JACQUES. *Jean Giono.* Paris-Bruxelles: Editions Universitaires, 1955. Concerned primarily with Giono's social philosophy, which this Leftist critic disapproves. Original, valuable interpretation of certain novels, however, as well as of the change in Giono's early and later manners.

ROBERT, PIERRE. *Jean Giono et les techniques du roman.* Berkeley and Los Angeles: University of California Press, 1961. As the title suggests, somewhat technical in nature; has clearly stated insights into the ways Giono has modernized his technique as a novelist.

ROCHE, ALPHONSE. "Les Provencialismes et la question du régionalisme dans l'œuvre de Jean Giono." *Publications of the Modern Language Association*, LXIII (1948), 1322–43. Professor Roche, for-merly of Northwestern and now of Arizona University, is himself a native of Provence and is well equipped for this study of Giono's style.

ROUSSEAUX, ANDRÉ. "Jean Giono, seconde manière," *Figaro Littéraire* (May 7, 1953), p. 2. This critic, very unfavorable in his articles concerning Giono's earlier work, is enthusiastic in his preference for Giono's post-war development, particularly *Le Hussard sur le toit.*

SMITH, MAXWELL A. "A Visit to Giono," *Books Abroad.* XXXIII (Winter, 1959), 23–6. A rather intimate glimpse of Giono's appearance, surroundings, and attitude towards his work.

STARR, W. T. "Jean Giono and Walt Whitman," *The French Review,* XIV (Dec., 1941), 118–29. Of special interest to students of American literature.

VIAL, FERNAND. "Jean Giono at the Académie Goncourt." *The American Society Legion of Honor Magazine.* (Spring, 1955), pp. 9–25. An interesting account of Giono's election to the Goncourt Academy together with a general survey of his career and works.

VILLENEUVE, ROMÉE DE. *Jean Giono, ce solitaire.* Avignon: Presses Universelles, 1955. Although the writer's admiration for Giono is somewhat uncritical, this is a valuable work. It is most comprehensive, including all of Giono's work, even his plays and essays. The writer was fortunate in having access to Giono's unpublished diary.

WALKER, HALLAM. "Myth in Giono's *Le Chant du monde.*" *Symposium,* XV (Summer, 1961), 139–46. Excellent study of Giono's capacity for creation of myth as an epic novelist.

Index

Index

Index

DATE DUE

GAYLORD			PRINTED IN U.S.A.